A Crash Course in SPSS FOR WINDOWS

A Crash Course in SPSS for Windows

Rod Corston and Andrew Colman

The right of Rod Corston and Andrew M. Colman to be identified as authors of this work
has been asserted in accordance with the Copyright, Designs and Patents Act 1988.

First published 2000

2 4 6 8 10 9 7 5 3 1

Blackwell Publishers Ltd
108 Cowley Road
Oxford OX4 1JF
UK

Blackwell Publishers Inc.
350 Main Street
Malden, Massachusetts 02148
USA

British Library Cataloguing in Publication Data

A CIP catalogue record for this book is available
from the British Library.

Library of Congress Cataloging-in-Publication Data has been applied for

ISBN 0–631–21770–3 (hbk.)
ISBN 0–631–21771–1 (pbk.)

Commissioning Editor: Martin Davies
Desk Editor: Tessa Hanford
Production Controller: Rhonda Pearce
Text Designer: Rhonda Pearce

Typeset in 10 on 12pt Galliard
by Graphicraft Limited, Hong Kong
Printed in Great Britain by TJ International, Padstow, Cornwall.

This book is printed on acid-free paper

Contents

Preface

With the help of this book, you should be able to learn SPSS for Windows quickly and painlessly, provided that you have some background knowledge of statistics. The package is fairly straightforward to use, and the basics can be explained without fuss. In our experience, busy people dislike spending large amounts of time learning computer applications. We believe that there is an important gap in the market arising from the fact that existing SPSS manuals are far more cumbersome and time-consuming than they need to be. Learning to use SPSS for Windows with such a manual is not only an unnecessary waste of time but also quite an ordeal. This book is designed to make things quicker and easier. It is based on an unpublished manual that we designed for undergraduate statistics courses. To a degree, therefore, it grew out of a specific need, and it proved popular because it fulfilled its intended function. We think that it deserves a wider readership.

The detailed procedures in this book are for users running Windows 95 or a later version of Windows and either SPSS 8 or SPSS 9 for Windows – other versions of Windows and of SPSS for Windows require slightly different operations, but most of the essential features of the package remain the same. All computational examples are taken from real data from published research, rather than hypothetical examples such as are found in most statistics and computing books, but we have chosen small data sets to avoid the task of inputting the data from becoming boring.

The first two chapters are written with complete beginners in mind. They describe the basic features of Windows and explain from the very beginning how to get the SPSS package up and running. If you already have some familiarity with Windows from using other Windows-based packages, then we suggest that you skim these introductory chapters quickly, paying attention to the useful new information in sections 2.4 and 2.6. Chapter 3 describes how data are loaded from disk and printed in SPSS for Windows. The remaining chapters describe the most widely used statistical techniques and graphic facilities available in SPSS for Windows. All of the procedures described in this book, with the sole exception of repeated-measures analysis of variance (chapter 11), are included in the SPSS for Windows Base System, and any computer on which SPSS for Windows is installed will run them.

Repeated-measures analysis of variance is available only if the SPSS Advanced Statistics add-on enhancement is also installed, but we decided to include it in this book because it is widely used, especially in the behavioural sciences.

An earlier draft of this book was road-tested by a number of students and academics who had expressed a wish to learn SPSS for Windows but, in most cases, had no previous knowledge or experience of it. Fifteen readers at a dozen different universities were sent a draft version of the book and were asked to work through it carefully, making a note of anything that they found unclear or that they felt could be improved, keeping a record of the time needed to complete the course. The responses of the readers to the draft were extremely encouraging, and most of them came up with numerous suggestions for every chapter. These suggestions enabled us to produce a revised version incorporating many improvements. The time taken by the end-users who took part in the usability trials ranged from five and a half to about nine hours, with a mean of just under seven hours (6 hours 52 minutes, to be exact), usually spread out over several sessions. Using this book, you should therefore be able to learn the basics of SPSS for Windows comfortably within ten hours.

We are grateful to everyone who took part in the usability trials, and to others who have offered technical advice and help of various kinds. In particular, we wish to express our gratitude to the following: Joseph Amoah-Nyako, John Armstrong, John Beckett, Mark Bowers, Kenneth Cowley, Simon Dunkley, Joanne Emery, Sarah Fishburn, Gerry Gardner, Erica Grossman, Rob Hemmings, Richard Joiner, Geoff Lowe, Sandy MacRae, Ian Pountney, Carolyn Preston, Briony Pulford, Kathy Smith, Helga Sneddon, David Stretch, Catherine Sugden, and Sue Wilson.

We have made the book as helpful as possible, but we weren't able to make it totally idiot-proof, partly because it would have been impossible and partly because only an idiot would want to read an idiot-proof book. But we've done our best to make it clear, explicit, and user-friendly, and we'd very much appreciate hearing from students and researchers about any further improvements that might be worth introducing into future editions. We'll acknowledge everyone who offers helpful suggestions unless they ask us not to. Please e-mail us or write to us care of the publisher.

Rod Corston (rcorston@cwcom.net)
Andrew Colman (amc@le.ac.uk)

CHOOSING AN APPROPRIATE STATISTICAL PROCEDURE

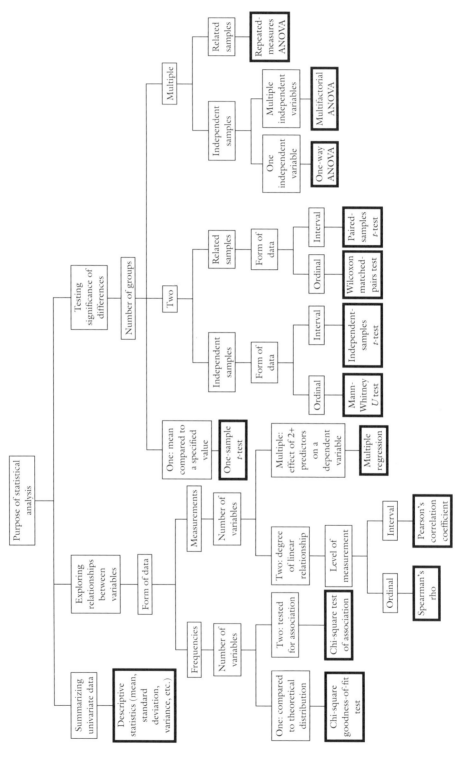

WHERE TO FIND THINGS IN SPSS

Procedure	*Menu location*
Analysis of variance	*See* Multifactorial analysis of variance, One-way analysis of variance, Repeated-measures analysis of variance
ANOVA	*See* Multifactorial analysis of variance, One-way analysis of variance, Repeated-measures analysis of variance
Charts and graphs	Graphs Bar . . ./ Line . . ./ Area . . ./ Pie . . . etc.

Chi-square goodness-of-fit test	Statistics (or Analyze)
	    Nonparametric Tests
	        Chi-Square . . .

Chi-square test of association	Statistics (or Analyze)
	    Summarize (or Descriptive Statistics)
	        Crosstabs . . .

Correlation	*See* Pearson's correlation coefficient, Spearman's rho

Descriptive statistics	Statistics (or Analyze)
	    Summarize (or Descriptive Statistics)
	        Frequencies . . ./ Descriptives . . . etc.

Goodness of fit	*See* Chi-square goodness-of-fit test
Graphs	*See* Charts and graphs

Independent-samples *t*-test	Statistics (or Analyze)
	    Compare Means
	        Independent-Samples T-Test . . .

Mann-Whitney *U* test	Statistics (or Analyze)
	    Nonparametric Tests
	        2 Independent Samples . . .

Matched-groups *t*-test	*See* Paired-samples *t*-test

Mean	Statistics (or Analyze)
	    Summarize (or Descriptive Statistics)
	        Descriptives . . .

Multifactorial analysis of variance	Statistics (or Analyze)
	    General Linear Model
	        GLM – General Factorial . . . (or Univariate . . .)

Multiple regression	Statistics (or Analyze)
	    Regression
	        Linear . . .

Procedure	Menu location

One-sample *t*-test	Statistics (or Analyze)
	    Compare Means
	        One-Sample T-Test . . .

One-way analysis of variance	Statistics (or Analyze)
	    Compare Means
	        One-Way ANOVA . . .

Paired-samples *t*-test	Statistics (or Analyze)
	    Compare Means
	        Paired-Samples T-Test . . .

Pearson's correlation coefficient	Statistics (or Analyze)
	    Correlate
	        Bivariate . . .

Related-groups *t*-test	*See* Paired-samples *t*-test

Repeated-measures analysis of variance	Statistics (or Analyze)
	    General Linear Model
	        GLM Repeated Measures . . .

Rho	*See* Spearman's rho

Spearman's rho	Statistics (or Analyze)
	    Correlate
	        Bivariate . . .

Standard deviation	Statistics (or Analyze)
	    Summarize (or Descriptive Statistics)
	        Descriptives . . .

t-test	*See* Independent-samples *t*-test, One-sample *t*-test, Paired-samples *t*-test
U test	*See* Mann-Whitney *U* test

Variance	Statistics (or Analyze)
	    Summarize (or Descriptive Statistics)
	        Descriptives . . .

Wilcoxon matched-pairs test	Statistics (or Analyze)
	    Nonparametric Tests
	        2 Independent Samples . . .

Wilcoxon signed-ranks test	*See* Wilcoxon matched-pairs test

1 Introduction

SPSS is an abbreviation of Statistical Product and Service Solutions (formerly Statistical Package for the Social Sciences), and it is distributed by SPSS Inc. of Chicago, Illinois, USA. Releases 8 and 9 of SPSS for Windows run on the Microsoft Windows 95 platform and later versions of Windows, and the detailed operations described in this book apply specifically to these versions. For other versions of Windows and of SPSS, there are slight variations, but most of the essential features remain the same.

SPSS for Windows is one of the oldest and most popular of the many packages of computer programs currently available for statistical analysis. Although it is extremely powerful, it is relatively easy to use once you have been taught the rudiments. We can teach you the rudiments quite quickly, and you will certainly need some guidance, because the package is not self-explanatory and you cannot simply teach yourself to use it from its help menu, as one of us tried unsuccessfully to do. For both of us, and for many people we've spoken to, the chief problem in learning to use it was that the various manuals on the market – some issued by SPSS Inc. and some by independent writers – were too detailed, too complicated, and above all too *long* to provide the quick introduction that we needed. This book is aimed at readers like ourselves who lack the time to plough through thick manuals, or the patience to submit to a screen-based tutor, but who want to be able to pick up the essential skills for performing standard statistical analyses with SPSS for Windows, and who prefer to learn these skills rapidly and painlessly. If you are one of those people who *are* happy to spend many evenings and weekends learning SPSS for Windows the long way, then our considered advice to you is that you should get out more and develop some leisure activities.

Chapter 2 will begin with a general introduction to the use of Windows, concentrating on the essential skills required for using SPSS for Windows. If you are already familiar with Windows, you can safely skip most of the elementary information in chapter 2, but you should read sections 2.4 and 2.6 to learn how to enter and save data in SPSS for Windows. The chapters that follow will tell you how to load data from disk, how to print data, how to obtain descriptive statistics, including means, standard deviations, and variances, how to compute Pearson's correlation coefficient and Spearman's rho, chi-square tests, t-tests for independent and paired samples, Mann–Whitney U tests, Wilcoxon matched-pairs tests, analysis of variance in all its major forms, and multiple regression, and how to draw charts and graphs with SPSS for Windows. The procedures covered by this book include the most important ones used in psychology and the social and behavioural sciences generally. Once you have mastered these techniques, you should have little difficulty teaching yourself the many other procedures available in SPSS for Windows.

This book will not teach you statistics. We assume that you already know enough about statistics to understand what assumptions are made about the data that you enter into SPSS for Windows, what procedures to use for analysing the data, and how to interpret the results. There is no point trying to analyse data unless you know what you are doing. If you need to brush up on your basic knowledge of statistics, there are many good books for you to consult. Among the ones that we're happy to recommend are Hays (1994), Howell (1999), Huck and Cormier (1996), and Pagano (1998). (Bibliographic details of publications cited in the text can all be found in the list of references at the back of this book.) We have none the less included in this book on page x a flow chart to help readers choose an appropriate statistical procedure, and a table on pages xi–xii showing where to find things in SPSS for Windows. Both are restricted to only the most commonly used procedures that are specifically dealt with in this book. There are far more statistical procedures available in SPSS for Windows, and both the flow chart and the table are only rudimentary, in the spirit of the book as a whole.

Even if you know what you're doing, the output that you obtain will be of little value if your data are of poor quality. This nugget of truth is expressed in the computer slang word *gigo*, which stands for garbage in, garbage out. Awesome though it is, SPSS for Windows is not a magic oven that can cook garbage input and miraculously transform it into *haute cuisine* output. To get useful output, you need properly collected data and carefully considered statistical analysis.

We hope and expect that this book will put you on the road to becoming a fluent and efficient user of SPSS for Windows. Believe it or not, data analysis can be fun. The results of our usability trials show that a crash course in SPSS for Windows using this book should take no more than about ten hours and should be quite enjoyable. Happy computing!

2 Using Windows

2.1 RUNNING SPSS FOR WINDOWS

We're going to show you how to use SPSS for Windows from scratch, but the first thing to do after switching on your computer and its monitor (screen) is to run Windows, and then you must run the SPSS statistics package. How you do this depends on how your computer has been configured. When the computer is switched on, it may boot up directly into Windows, or to a menu of options, or to the Microsoft DOS prompt.

◆ If your computer boots up to a menu that includes an option to select Windows, press the space bar or the keyboard cursor keys (the four keys marked with little arrows pointing left, right, up, and down, respectively) until the Windows option is highlighted on the screen, and then press ENTER – the large key on the right of the keyboard labelled ENTER, RETURN, CR (for carriage return), or marked ↵.

◆ If your computer boots up to the DOS prompt, usually **C:\>**, but possibly with a different letter in place of the C, type the starting command (usually **win** or **exit**) and then press the ENTER key to start Windows.

◆ If your computer boots up to a login prompt, usually **F:\LOGIN>**, though again the letter may be different, type a username, press ENTER, then type a password and press ENTER again. If you haven't got a username and password, seek help.

Depending on your particular setup, you may have to use some other procedure for running Windows. Once Windows is running, the screen will initially show the Windows desktop, with a **Start** button in its bottom-left corner, and there are two main ways in which you may run SPSS for Windows from there.

1. Slide the mouse across a pad or some suitable surface until the arrow-shaped mouse pointer on the screen is on the **Start** button in the lower-left corner of the screen, and click the left-hand mouse button once. From now on, whenever we refer to the mouse button without saying which one, we'll mean the left-hand mouse button. Alternatively, if you have a Windows keyboard, you may press either of the Windows keys near the space bar. In the pop-up list that appears, use the mouse or the keyboard cursor keys to highlight **Programs**, and then, while **Programs** is highlighted, activate the submenu of programs by pressing the right-pointing cursor key or by using the mouse.

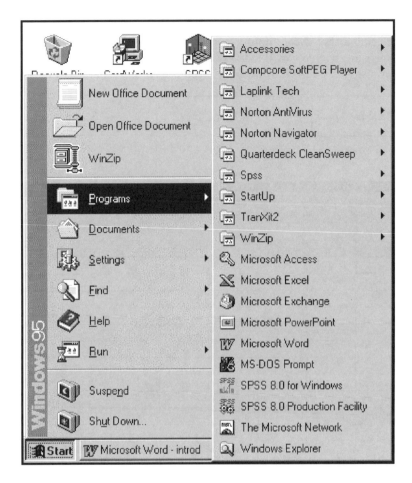

Use the cursor keys or mouse to highlight **SPSS 8.0 for Windows** or **SPSS 9.0 for Windows** in the submenu, then either click the mouse or press the ENTER key. This will start the program running, and after a few seconds you will see the Data Editor, which we'll show you after describing the second method of accessing SPSS for Windows.

2. The Windows desktop may display a number of small boxes containing little icons (pictures), and one of these may be labelled SPSS. Icons such as these are hidden once a program is launched.

If you see the SPSS icon, you can launch SPSS for Windows directly with the mouse. Double-click the SPSS icon (click twice in rapid succession), and wait a few seconds while the mouse pointer turns itself temporarily into an hour-glass, indicating that the computer is busy loading the SPSS statistics package.

Eventually, SPSS for Windows will be up and running, and you'll know that it is because after a brief introductory screen display the SPSS Data Editor will appear.

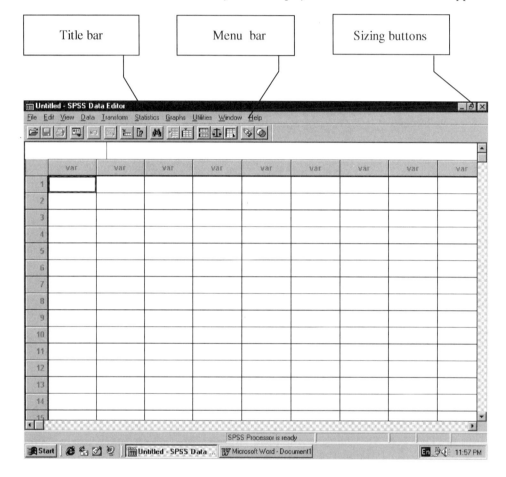

2.2 RESIZING AND MOVING A WINDOW

When SPSS for Windows starts up, the screen will display the SPSS Data Editor. It is divided into columns and rows and is captioned (in its title bar at the top) **Untitled – SPSS Data Editor**. Immediately below the title bar is a menu bar:

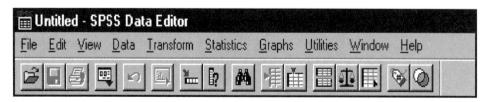

For the time being, ignore the various odds and ends in the menu bar and the icon bar below it; we'll tell you what these things mean as and when you need them. But do notice the word **Help** on the right. You can click it with the mouse whenever you like, and you may find it useful if you need to look something up in the help menu. Many of the dialog boxes that you'll encounter in the chapters that follow have specialized help buttons that are often more useful because they are context-specific: they supply information just about the particular job you are doing at the time. (The right-hand mouse button often serves a similar function.) Feel free to click the help buttons whenever you feel helpless, or even just curious; they won't necessarily solve your problem, unfortunately, but at least you'll always be able to get back to where you were before by clicking the small black cross in the top-right corner of the help topic box.

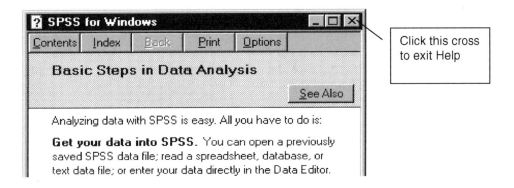

Having introduced you to the notion of windows, we'll show you how to resize and move a window. First of all, to alter the size of a window you must click one of the buttons that appear near the top-right corner of most windows:

- ◆ To *minimize* a window – that is, to close it down and place its icon at the bottom of the screen – click the small dash on the left. Try it now, and after minimizing it, restore it by clicking the SPSS Data Editor icon in the bar at the very bottom of the Windows desktop.
- ◆ To *tile* the windows – to reduce the currently active window and reveal any other working windows lurking behind it – click the overlapping rectangles in the middle. Try it now, and notice that the Data Editor window is reduced in size and the only other working window is the Windows desktop in the background, because you haven't done any analysis or drawn any charts or graphs.

◆ You can *move* a window across the screen to a new position, but this is possible only if it has first been reduced in size. Click its title bar and hold the mouse button down instead of releasing it. With the mouse button held down, drag the mouse across a surface until the window is where you want it to be, and then release the button. Try moving the reduced Data Editor window now.

Notice that when you reduced the size of the Data Editor window, the middle button in the top-right corner of the screen changed from overlapping rectangles to a single rectangle:

◆ To *maximize* a window that has been reduced in size – to restore it so that it fills the whole screen – click the single rectangle in the middle. Restore the Data Editor to its full size now.
◆ If you wanted to *close* the window and shut down the program, you could click the cross on the right, but don't do it now, because we have more to tell you about the Data Editor.

2.3 THE DATA EDITOR

As long as the Data Editor window is active, you can enter data into SPSS. We'll give you a small data set to enter by hand. The scores come from a well-known Danish study of the IQ scores of 12 pairs of identical twins separated early in life and raised in different homes (Juel-Nielsen, 1965).

Twin A:	119	99	108	91	111	105	100	91	104	125	111	99
Twin B:	121	103	97	100	117	97	94	98	103	111	117	112

To compute any statistics for this data set, you must first enter the scores into the Data Editor, which is essentially a spreadsheet – an array of rows and columns extending downwards and to the right, far beyond what you can see on the screen. Its rows are labelled **1, 2, 3**, and so on, and its columns are all initially labelled **var** (short for variable). For some types of analysis in SPSS, data must be set out with each group of scores, or each variable, in a separate column. For other types of analysis, the data must be arranged in a single column, with one score per row, even if they come from two or more groups. We'll return to this complication in section 4.3. For now, we'll show you how to enter the 12 pairs of IQ scores in the natural way, in two separate columns.

The first column will contain the IQ scores labelled *Twin A* in the table and the second column the scores labelled *Twin B*. Beginning at the beginning, the first column will contain, from top to bottom, the numbers 119, 99, 108, and so on, and the second column will contain the numbers 121, 103, 97, and so on. The data will be set out as follows, once you have keyed them into the Data Editor.

	twina	twinb	var
1	119.00	121.00	
2	99.00	103.00	
3	108.00	97.00	
4	91.00	100.00	
5	111.00	117.00	
6	105.00	97.00	
7	100.00	94.00	
8	91.00	98.00	
9	104.00	103.00	
10	125.00	111.00	
11	111.00	117.00	
12	99.00	112.00	
13			
14			
15			

So how do you key the scores in? It isn't as straightforward as you may expect, but it isn't difficult either. You should first name the variables so that the output is properly labelled and understandable.

◆ Double-click the word **var** at the top of the first column, and the Define Variable dialog box will open.

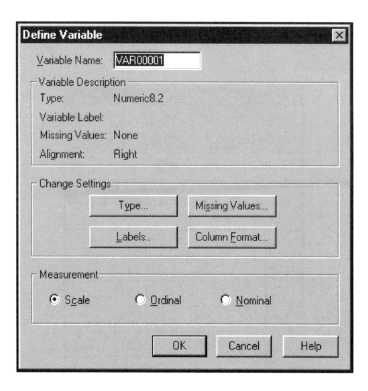

In the Define Variable dialog box you can give the first variable a sensible name. Inside the dialog box, the text box labelled **Variable Name** shows the default name of the first variable: VAR00001. This isn't an inspiring variable name, and it won't be very helpful when you read the output, so you may want to rename it **Juel-Nielsen Twins (A)**, or **Twin #A** or something similar, but unfortunately there are constraints on variable names. A variable name must not exceed eight characters, which must be letters, numbers, or certain other characters, but not spaces, and it must begin with a letter. So let's call the first set of scores **twina**.

◆ Just type **twina** in the **Variable Name** text box and the default name VAR00001 will disappear and be replaced by this new name. If you clicked the **Help** button or used the right-hand mouse button, you'd find out about the various other items in this dialog box, but none of them is terribly important at this stage.

◆ Now that you have finished naming this variable, click **OK**, and after a pause you'll be back in the Data Editor, where you'll find that the first column is no longer headed **var** but is now reassuringly headed **twina**.

◆ To name the second variable, double-click **var** at the top of the second column, and rename this variable **twinb** using the same procedure. Click **OK**. You're now ready to key in the data.

2.4   ENTERING DATA

You can't type your raw scores directly into the cells of the Data Editor, and this always puzzles people at first. As you type in the scores, they appear initially in an area called the cell editor just below the Data Editor's icon bar. Once you have typed a number and it has appeared there, press ENTER to transfer it to one of the cells below. The score will then jump into the active cell – the one that is currently highlighted with a black border.

◆ Before entering the first number, make sure that the correct cell, namely **1:twina**, is highlighted. To highlight it, simply click inside it.

◆ Use the number keys at the top of the keyboard or, if you prefer to use the numeric keypad on the right, make sure that the number lock (Num Lock) is on. Enter the first score from the Twin A group, which happens to be 119, by typing it into the cell editor and then pressing ENTER. After a pause (do give SPSS a moment to collect its thoughts when you enter your first score), the score will jump into the first cell and the highlight will move to the next cell down. You could enter the score 99 here, because that is the second score from the Twin A group.

◆ Depending on the order in which you want to enter the data, you may find it more convenient to press one of the cursor keys rather than ENTER after typing a number into the cell editor. For example, after typing the first score, if instead of pressing ENTER you press the right-pointing cursor key, then the first number will be transferred to the first row of the first column exactly as before, but the next cell to be highlighted will be the one immediately to the right of it (**1:twinb**), where you could enter 121 (the first score from the Twin B group) before moving on to the second row, where the next pair of IQ scores need to be entered. Use whichever method suits you best.

◆ Use the cursor keys to move around the Data Editor if you find yourself in the wrong place. If at any point you find that the wrong cell is highlighted, you can highlight the correct cell by clicking inside it.

◆ If, after entering some or all of the data, you find that you have made a mistake, highlight the offending cell by clicking inside it, and then simply enter the new number in the cell editor and press ENTER. The new entry will replace the old. To delete the contents of any cell, highlight the cell and press the DELETE (Del) key. To delete a whole column, click the grey area at the top of the column where its name appears, so that the whole column is highlighted, and then press the DELETE key. You can highlight and delete a whole row in the same way, by clicking in a numbered row of the grey border on the left.

2.5   SCROLLING

As you enter data, the Data Editor will fill up, and if you have more data than can fit in the ten rows and seven columns of the window, then some of the data will scroll out of sight. For example, some of the data that you entered in section 2.4 may have scrolled off the top of the window if you have a small screen. If you need to examine data that have disappeared from view, you can do this either with the cursor keys or the mouse.

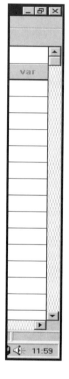

- ◆ *Using the cursor keys.* To see information that has scrolled off the top of the window, press the **up** cursor key, and the hidden information will reappear. To scroll down again, press the **down** cursor key. You may also scroll to the left and right by using the **left** and **right** cursor keys, but no left-right scrolling is necessary with the data you have just entered because there were not enough columns for anything to have scrolled off to the left.
- ◆ *Using the mouse.* The right-hand border of the Data Editor window is actually a scroll bar – this is a standard feature of many Windows applications.

  At the top of the scroll bar is an arrow pointing up, at the bottom is an arrow pointing down, and between the two is a square grey block. To scroll, click the block and, with the mouse button held down, drag the block up or down, then release the mouse button, and the display will scroll, assuming that there are some data off the screen to scroll to. This is a slightly awkward manoeuvre, and there's another method. You may find it easier to click on the scroll arrow at the top or bottom of the scroll bar, and the display will scroll up or down as long as the mouse button is being held down. There is a similar scroll bar with its own scroll arrows and block in the bottom border of the Data Editor window, and it can be used in exactly the same way for scrolling to the left or right if there are enough columns of input data to have caused the display to have scrolled off to the left.

2.6 SAVING DATA ON DISK

Having entered data into SPSS, you will often want to save the data on disk for future analysis or re-analysis. Depending on the machine you're using, you may or may not be able to save the data on the computer's hard drive, but you can normally save a file on a floppy disk instead. This is generally more convenient, because you can take the disk away with you, so we'll show you how to do that.

- ◆ First, make sure that the Data Editor window has the data you want to save in it.
- ◆ Insert a floppy disk into the disk drive (usually called drive A).

◆ Click the word **File** in the menu bar at the top of the Data Editor window. A drop-down file menu will appear.

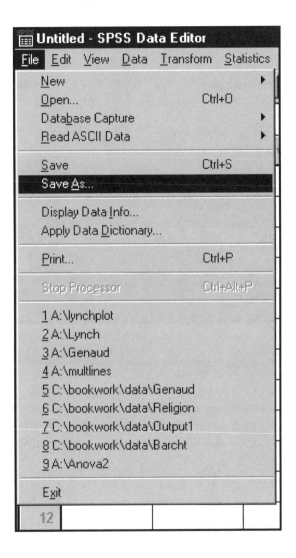

◆ Provided that the Data Editor has some data in it, the command **Save As...** will be shown in black. Menu items that are dimmed – displayed tantalizingly in light grey – are currently unavailable. Use the mouse or the cursor arrows to highlight **Save As...**, then click it and a dialog box called Save Data As will appear. It's worth pointing out that SPSS menu commands followed by three dots (...) always open dialog boxes, and menu commands followed by an arrowhead (▶) always open submenus.

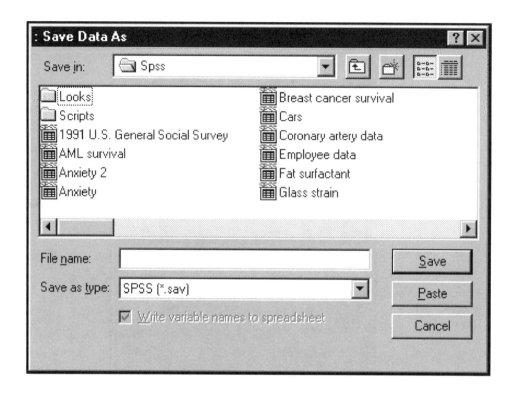

- ◆ Now tell the computer on which drive to save your data. By default, the text box labelled **Save in** near the top of this dialog box will probably be showing **Spss**, but you are not going to save your data within SPSS. Click the little black arrow on the right of the text box, and a drop-down list will appear. Assuming that you have a standard floppy disk, use the mouse or the cursor arrows to highlight **3½ Floppy (A:)** and click it or press the ENTER key so that it appears in the text box.

- ◆ Next, give the file a name. Click in the text box labelled **File name**, and type a suitable filename. A filename must begin with a letter but need not be restricted to eight characters, as in earlier versions of SPSS, and it may now include spaces. A filename is normally followed by a full stop and a three-letter extension, which in the case of an SPSS input data file should be **.sav**. The filename (one word) together with its extension is called a file name (two words). We suggest that you use the file name **twinsiq.sav**.

- ◆ Make sure that the text box labelled **Save as type** is showing **SPSS(*.sav)**. If it isn't, then click the little black arrow on the right of the text box, and a drop-down list will appear. Use the mouse or the cursor arrows to highlight **SPSS(*.sav)**, and click it or press the ENTER key so that it appears in the text box. This ensures that your data will be saved in SPSS format.

- ◆ To save the file, click the **Save** button in the dialog box and wait for the data to be saved before removing your disk. There may be a little light on the computer that goes out when the floppy disk stops spinning. Save the file now, because you'll need to retrieve it for chapters 3 and 4 – saving it at this point will mean that you won't have to key the data in again later.

2.7   EXITING **SPSS** FOR WINDOWS

At the end of your work session, you should exit from SPSS in an orderly fashion. You do this via the **File** drop-down menu.

◆ Click **File** in the menu bar at the top of the Data Editor window.
◆ Click **Exit** at the bottom of the menu.

If you haven't saved your data, a message will be displayed asking you whether you want to save the contents of the Data Editor. You can then either save your data as described in section 2.6 and exit SPSS or exit directly if you have saved the information previously or are happy to discard it.

3 Loading Data from Disk and Printing

3.1 LOADING DATA FROM DISK

It is not always necessary to key in data by hand. If you have a data file stored on disk or accessible from a web site, you can load it directly into SPSS for analysis. Here's how to load the input data from chapter 2 into the Data Editor.

◆ First, run SPSS in the usual way from Windows (see section 2.1). When SPSS starts up, the Data Editor window will initially be active.

◆ Click **File** in the menu bar near the top of the Data Editor window. Incidentally, you can open any of the menus in the menu bar without using the mouse, by holding down the Alt key and typing the underlined letter (in this case F).

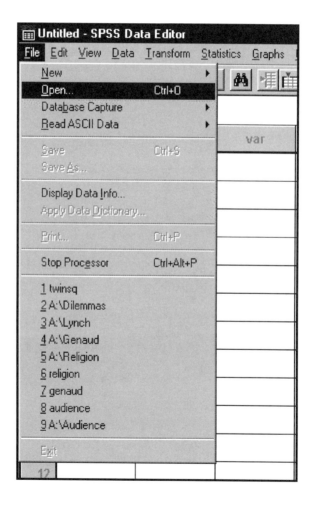

◆ In the drop-down menu, click the command **Open...** and the Open File dialog box will appear. Alternatively, you can always execute a menu command by simply typing its underlined letter, in this case O, without holding down the Alt key.

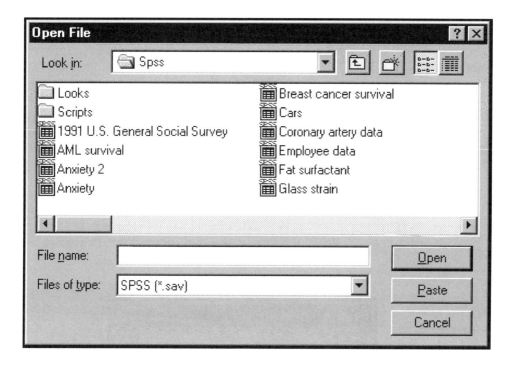

◆ Assuming that the data you want to load are on the A drive, go to the text box labelled **Look in**, open its drop-down menu by clicking the arrow on its right, and click **3½ Floppy (A:)** in the list of options displayed. The text box will now show **3½ Floppy (A:)**.

◆ Choose the file you want by clicking its name in the Open File dialog box, which lists all SPSS data files on the A drive with the extension **.sav**. Use the scroll bar if necessary (see section 2.5). If your file is not an ordinary SPSS data file, then you must specify something different in the **File of type** text box, but we needn't go into that now. The filename under which you saved the data in chapter 2 was **twinsiq**, and it was obviously a bog standard SPSS data file, so the filename should appear in the list. Select it by clicking it, and it will appear in the **File name** text box below.

◆ Once you are satisfied that you have selected the right file from the right drive, click **Open**. Messages will appear at the bottom of the screen to reassure you that SPSS is on the job, and in a few seconds the Data Editor will reappear with your data from chapter 2 loaded into it, exactly as if you had just entered the scores by hand. If for some reason you didn't save the file earlier, then at this point you should go back to sections 2.3 and 2.4 and key the data in by hand.

3.2 PRINTING AN ENTIRE DATA SET

At some stage you are bound to want to print a hard copy of some SPSS data. You may want a printout of input data in the Data Editor, or after you have analysed some data you may want a printout of the results of the analysis from the SPSS Viewer window, where the results are displayed. You will be able to print data only if your computer is connected to a suitable printer. What to do if the setup is wrong is beyond the scope of this crash course. Seek help. If a suitable printer is connected, then here's how to print your data. The procedure is essentially the same whether you are printing input or output data, so for now we'll print the input data from chapter 2 that you have just loaded up again, because sadly you haven't any output data yet, though you'll have some soon, we promise.

- ◆ Make sure that your data file is in the Data Editor.
- ◆ Open the **File** drop-down menu by clicking its name in the menu bar, then click the command **Print...**, and a dialog box called Print A:\twinsiq.sav will open.

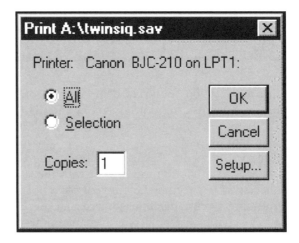

- ◆ To print the entire contents of the Data Editor, make sure that the radio button marked **All** is lit up. If it isn't, click it. Round buttons of this type are called radio buttons because, like the buttons on a car radio, only one can be selected at a time.
- ◆ Click **OK**, and the data will be printed pronto. Try it now.
- ◆ At a later stage, when you come to print output from SPSS calculations, you will get a slightly different Print dialog box.

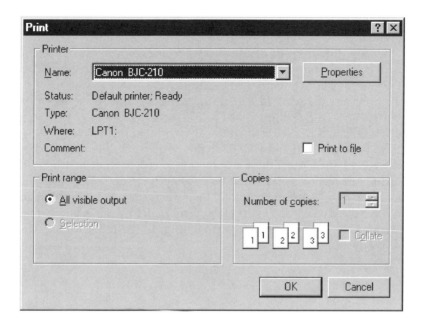

You will use the radio button in this dialog box to choose to print the visible output or a selection (see below), and you can choose the number of copies that you require.

3.3 PRINTING A SELECTION OF DATA

There may be times when you need to print only some of the input or output data in an SPSS window. To print a selection of the data that you have just loaded, proceed as follows.

◆ In the case of input data in the Data Editor, select the data that you want to print by the click-and-drag technique. Click the mouse with its pointer at the beginning of the block of data that you want to select and, with the mouse button held down, drag the pointer to the end of the block, then release the mouse button. If you click a variable name at the top of a column in the Data Editor, then the whole column will be selected automatically, and you can do the same thing with a row. If you need to include data that have scrolled off the screen and you're using the click-and-drag technique, then go carefully as the mouse pointer nears the edge of the window, and the hidden data will automatically scroll into view. The selected block of data (apart from the cell that is already highlighted with a black border) will be highlighted in black – perhaps we should say lowlighted. If you find that you've made a mistake and selected something you didn't intend to, then just click in a blank area of the screen outside the marked block and the highlight will vanish. Select some of the input data on twins' IQ scores now. In the case of output data in the

SPSS Viewer, you can select a single table or graphic object by clicking once inside it.

♦ Open the **File** drop-down menu by clicking its name in the menu bar, and then click the command **Print...**, and the dialog box called Print A:\twinsiq.sav that we showed you before will appear.

♦ To print just the selected data in the active window, make sure that the radio button marked **Selection** is lit up. If it isn't, click it.

♦ Click **OK**, and the selected data will be printed out for you.

♦ If you want to exit from SPSS at this stage, click **File** in the menu bar near the top of the Data Editor window, followed by **Exit** at the bottom of the menu (see section 2.7). You'll be needing the twins' data again in chapter 4, so if you didn't save them before, then when a dialog box appears inviting you to save the data, click **Yes** and save them under the file name **twinsiq.sav** (see section 2.6). If you want to go straight on to the next chapter, keep the data in the Data Editor.

4 General Descriptive Statistics

4.1 ANALYSING DATA

Now at last you're ready for some actual data analysis. You'll begin with general descriptive statistics, then in later chapters you'll move on to correlations and inferential statistics.

To calculate general descriptive statistics, you obviously need a set of data entered in the Data Editor. To save time and conserve energy, we suggest that you use the data that you saved on disk in chapter 2 under the file name **twinsiq.sav**. Load the data set into the Data Editor by following the procedure explained in section 3.1. If you still haven't got this file on disk, then go to sections 2.3 and 2.4 and key the data in by hand.

4.2 MEANS, STANDARD DEVIATIONS, ETC.

Now you can calculate, for each group, the mean, standard deviation, minimum, and maximum, and if you wish you can also calculate the sum, variance, range, standard error of the mean, kurtosis, and skewness of each group. This is how you do it.

◆ Once the data have been entered into the Data Editor, click **Statistics** (or **Analyze**) in the menu bar near the top of the Data Editor window. A drop-down menu will appear. Click the **Summarize** (or **Descriptive Statistics**) command on this menu.

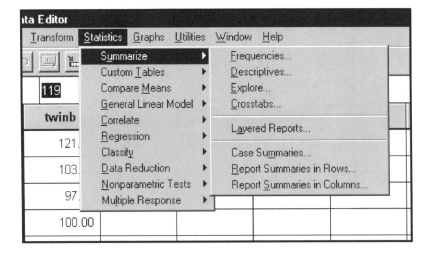

◆ When the **Summarize** (or **Descriptive Statistics**) submenu opens, click **Descriptives...**, and try to remember for next time that this is where to find basic descriptive statistics in SPSS, because it isn't obvious. The Descriptives dialog box will open.

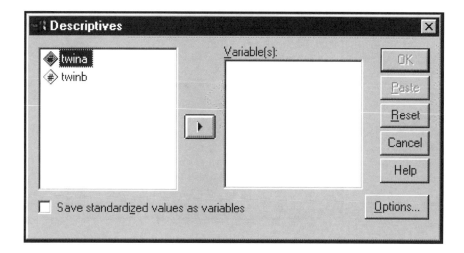

◆ In the Descriptives dialog box, the names of the variables in the data set are listed on the left, and on the right there is a box labelled **Variable(s)**. First move each of the variables for which you want descriptive statistics into the **Variable(s)** box by clicking its variable name to highlight it and then clicking the black arrow button pointing towards the **Variable(s)** box. The selected variable will shoot across into the **Variable(s)** box. If you make a mistake and want to move a variable back where it came from, then just select it in the right-hand box by clicking it and then click the arrow button, which will now obligingly be pointing to the left. Clicking the **Reset** button will restore all variables to their original places. For now, select both variables for analysis.

◆ If you wanted SPSS to convert the scores to standardized Z scores and to save them in that form, you could at this point click the check box beside **Save standardized values as variables**. This option is selected when a tick appears in its check box, and you can remove a tick by clicking again. There is no need for Z scores now.

◆ Click **Options...** at the bottom of the Descriptives dialog box to open a subdialog box in which you can specify which descriptive statistics to calculate..

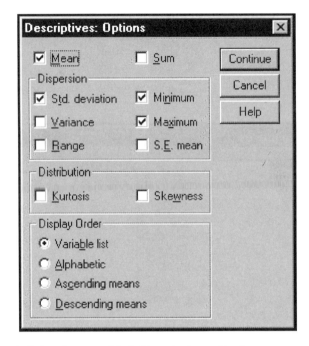

◆ When the subdialog box entitled Descriptives: Options opens, the options **Mean**, **Std. deviation** (standard deviation), **Minimum**, and **Maximum** are already selected by default, as shown by ticks in the check boxes alongside them. If you wished, you could select also **Sum**, **Variance**, **Range**, **S.E. mean** (standard error of the mean), **Kurtosis**, and **Skewness** by clicking their check boxes. It is also possible in the same dialog box to select the order in which the output data are displayed if this is important to you.

◆ Once you are satisfied that the options you want (for now, just the mean, standard deviation, minimum, and maximum), and only those, have been selected, click **Continue**. This will return you to the Descriptives dialog box.

◆ Now click **OK**, and after a pause the SPSS Viewer window will appear with the results. The descriptive statistics for each of the groups that you included in the analysis will be displayed separately. If some of the results scroll off the window, use the scroll bars as explained in section 2.5.

➡ Descriptives

Descriptive Statistics

	N	Minimum	Maximum	Mean	Std. Deviation
TWINA	12	91.00	125.00	105.2500	10.2967
TWINB	12	94.00	121.00	105.8333	9.3014
Valid N (listwise)	12				

The output is self-explanatory. For example, although they were separated early in life and raised in different homes, the Twin A and Twin B groups have almost identical mean IQs of 105.25 and 105.83, respectively. To print a hard copy of the output, follow the procedure described in section 3.2.

4.3 CUTTING AND PASTING

For certain analyses discussed in later chapters of this book, you will have to format the data with all of the scores in a single column, one score per row, and with a separate column containing a grouping variable indicating the group to which each score belongs. There are many other circumstances in which you may need to cut and paste. We'll show you now how to cut and paste the input data so that all the IQ scores are in a single column. First, return to the Data Editor window by clicking **Window** in the menu bar near the top of the SPSS Viewer window, and when the menu drops down clicking the window that you want to activate, which is of course the **SPSS Data Editor**.

◆ Select the 12 scores in the second column, labelled **twinb**, by clicking and dragging: place the mouse pointer on the first of the **twinb** scores, press the mouse button and hold it down while dragging the mouse pointer over the rest of the scores in that column, and only then release the mouse button. The **twinb** scores will be highlighted in black. You could achieve the same effect by simply clicking the **twinb** variable name at the top of the column, as we mentioned earlier, but it's useful to practise clicking and dragging.

◆ Click **Edit** in the menu bar.

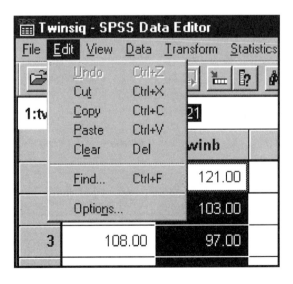

◆ From the Edit drop-down menu that appears, choose **Cut**. The **twinb** scores will vanish.

◆ Scroll down (see section 2.5) and select the next 12 empty cells (rows 13 to 24) below the **twina** scores in the first column of the Data Editor. Do this by clicking and dragging as before. These cells must be highlighted.

◆ Click **Edit** in the menu bar once more, but this time choose **Paste** from the drop-down Edit menu that appears. The scores from Group 2 will be pasted into the highlighted cells in the **twina** column.

◆ Now put a grouping variable in the second column. This is a feature of SPSS that you may as well start getting used to now. Let's use the code 1 for the group we called Twin A and 2 for Twin B – the grouping codes are arbitrary, and you could choose another pair of numbers if you wished. Scroll back to the top of the Data Editor, and in the second column type the number **1** into the first 12 cells (rows 1 to 12) and **2** into the next 12 cells (rows 13 to 24). Review section 2.4 if you've forgotten how to enter data by hand.

◆ Finally, use the following procedure to rename the variables that are now in the first two columns **iqscore** and **group**, respectively. Double-click **twina** at the top of the first column, and the Define Variable dialog box will open.

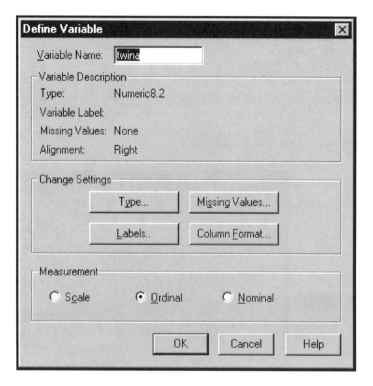

◆ Type **iqscore** to replace **twina** in the text box labelled **Variable Name**. If **twina** is not highlighted, because you did something else first, click in the text box and delete it with the Delete key before replacing it. Click **OK**.

◆ Back in the Data Editor, the first column will now be labelled **iqscore**, as it should be. Double-click **twinb** at the top of the second column. In the Define

Variable dialog box that opens, replace **twinb** with **group**, but before clicking **OK** give it value labels, because it is a grouping variable and SPSS needs to know what the labels 1 and 2 stand for. So click **Labels...** and the Define Labels subdialog box will open.

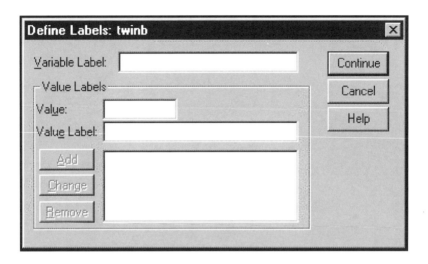

◆ Click inside the text box labelled **Value**, and type **1**, then click in the text box labelled **Value Label** and type **twina**. Click **Add**. In the box below, **1.00 =** "twina" will appear. Then repeat the process for the second value label. Click in the text box labelled **Value** and type **2**, then click in the box labelled **Value Label** and type **twinb**. Click **Add**. In the box below, **1.00 =** "twina" and **2.00 =** "twinb" will now both appear. In the same dialog box, if you were a forgetful type of person you could if you wished type a longer label, with spaces allowed, into the text box labelled **Variable label** to remind yourself that Twin A and Twin B are IQ scores of separated twins. Click **Continue**.

◆ Back in the Define Variable dialog box, click **OK**. Both columns are now named and the second is also properly labelled. This is how you would have to set out the data if you needed to perform an independent-samples *t*-test (section 7.2), for example.

◆ If you want to exit from SPSS at this point, click **File** in the menu bar near the top of the SPSS Viewer window, and then **Exit** at the bottom of the menu that drops down (see section 2.7). If you want to go straight on to the next chapter, click **File** in the menu bar, then **New**, then **Data**. There is no need to save the rearranged data set, unless you want to analyse the IQ scores later, so when a dialog box appears inviting you to save the data, click **No**, and an empty Data Editor will appear. If you do want to save the rearranged data for whatever reason, be sure to give it a new file name so as not to overwrite **twinsiq.sav**.

5 Correlation Coefficients

5.1 BACKGROUND

The correlation between two variables is the degree of (usually) linear relationship between them, such that high scores on one tend to go with high scores on the other or, in the case of negative correlation, such that high scores on one tend to go with low scores on the other. There are many different measures of correlation, including indices of nonlinear correlation, but the most common are measures of linear correlation called Pearson's product-moment correlation coefficient and Spearman's rho. Both of these coefficients range from 1.00 for perfect positive linear correlation, through zero for no linear correlation, to 1.00 for perfect negative linear correlation.

The most widely used index of all is Pearson's product-moment correlation coefficient. When social scientists refer to a correlation or a correlation coefficient without specifying the type, it is usually safe to assume that they are referring to Pearson's. Spearman's rho is a nonparametric version of Pearson's, designed for use with ordinal (ranked) data. In fact, from a mathematical point of view, Spearman's rho amounts to Pearson's product-moment correlation coefficient calculated after replacing the original scores by the ranks within each group. Section 5.2 will describe the procedure for calculating Pearson's product-moment correlation coefficient, and section 5.3 will outline how to calculate Spearman's rho.

5.2 PEARSON'S CORRELATION COEFFICIENT

Hovland and Sears (1940) analysed some unusual data in their research into the relationship between frustration and aggression. They compared the annual number of lynchings that took place in the southern United States from 1882 to 1930 with the value of cotton production in the corresponding years. They hypothesized that lynchings could be viewed as acts of displaced aggression that should be more numerous during periods of economic hardship for farmers in the cotton-producing southern states, when cotton production was low, than during periods of prosperity, when cotton production was high. The data were as shown in Table 5.1 overleaf.

◆ Enter the value of cotton production into the first column of the Data Editor and the numbers of lynchings into the second column, and name the two variables **cotton** and **lynch**, respectively. (If you've forgotten how to enter data or how to name variables, read sections 2.3 and 2.4 again.) There's no need to enter the dates, because they will not come into the calculation. If you had more than two variables you would enter each one in a separate column.

◆ Save the input data on disk for future reference by following the procedure described in section 2.6. Call the file **lynch.sav**.

◆ Click **Statistics** (or **Analyze**) in the menu bar near the top of the SPSS Data Editor window. Click **Correlate** in the drop-down menu that appears (see bottom of page 35).

Table 5.1 Cotton production and lynchings

Year	Cotton ($m)	Lynchings	Year	Cotton ($m)	Lynchings
1882	310	49	1907	614	60
1883	251	52	1908	589	93
1884	254	52	1909	688	73
1885	270	80	1910	810	65
1886	257	74	1911	750	63
1887	291	73	1912	787	61
1888	292	70	1913	863	50
1889	308	95	1914	549	49
1890	350	90	1915	631	54
1891	313	121	1916	1122	50
1892	268	155	1917	1566	36
1893	264	155	1918	1738	60
1894	259	134	1919	2020	76
1895	293	112	1920	1069	53
1896	292	80	1921	676	59
1897	319	122	1922	1116	51
1898	305	102	1923	1454	29
1899	325	84	1924	1561	16
1900	438	107	1925	1577	17
1901	381	107	1926	1121	23
1902	422	86	1927	1308	16
1903	576	86	1928	1302	10
1904	561	83	1929	1245	7
1905	557	61	1930	659	20
1906	640	65			

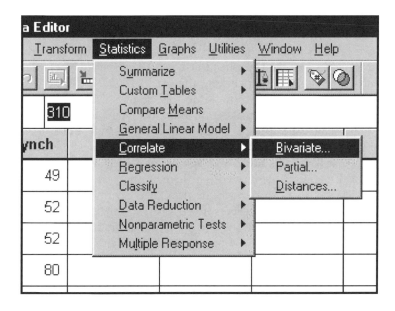

◆ Click **Bivariate...** in the submenu. This is the option for ordinary correlations between pairs of (bi-) variables. You could also have chosen **Partial...** for calculating partial correlations, which describe the relationship between two variables while controlling for a third – for example, the relationship between socioeconomic status and income among working people controlling for age. Or you could have chosen **Distances...** if you wanted to calculate various indices of similarity, dissimilarity, or distance. When you choose **Bivariate...**, the Bivariate Correlations dialog box will open.

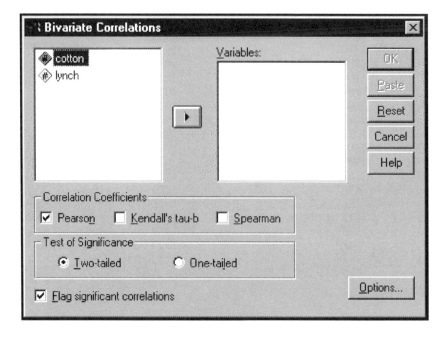

◆ The two variables that you have named **cotton** and **lynch** appear in the left-hand box. Move them to the right-hand box, which is labelled **Variables**, by clicking each of them and then clicking the black arrow button between the two boxes. (If you've forgotten how to do this, review section 4.2.)

◆ In the same dialog box, make sure that the type of correlation coefficient you want, namely **Pearson**, is selected. It is the default, but if for any reason the check box beside it doesn't have a tick inside it, click the check box. Make sure also that **Kendall's tau-b** and **Spearman**, which are nonparametric correlation coefficients, are deselected – if there are ticks in the check boxes beside them, click the boxes to remove the ticks. It is possible to choose more than one of the correlation coefficients if you wish, and that is why they have check boxes rather than radio buttons, but we're concentrating on Pearson's for the moment. We'll show you how to calculate Spearman's rho in section 5.3.

◆ Still in the Bivariate Correlations dialog box, select the test of significance you want to be applied to the correlation coefficient. **Two-tailed** is the default, but you could choose **One-tailed** if you wished by clicking its radio button. In order to cause correlation coefficients significant at the 0.05 level to be flagged with a single asterisk and coefficients significant at the 0.01 level with a double asterisk, make sure there's a tick in the check box beside **Flag significant correlations**. If this option is deselected (without a tick in its check box), then the output will still indicate the numerical values of the correlation coefficient and its significance level but will not asterisk the correlation if it is significant.

◆ The dialog box has a button labelled **Options...**, and if you clicked it, a subdialog box would open in which you could instruct SPSS to calculate means, standard deviations, cross-product deviations, and covariances. You would also be able to select a method of dealing with missing values, if you had any. The system default for handling missing values is to exclude cases pairwise, that is, to exclude from the calculation any cases (rows) with a missing value in either column.

◆ When you are satisfied that everything in the Bivariate Correlations dialog box is as you want it to be, click the **OK** button, and the SPSS Viewer window will appear, displaying the results. If some of the results scroll off the window, use the scroll bars as explained in section 2.5.

◆ If you want to print a hard copy of the output, follow the procedure described in section 3.2.

Correlations

Correlations

		COTTON	LYNCH
COTTON	Pearson Correlation	1.000	-.636**
	Sig. (2-tailed)	.	.000
	N	49	49
LYNCH	Pearson Correlation	-.636**	1.000
	Sig. (2-tailed)	.000	.
	N	49	49

**. Correlation is significant at the 0.01 level (2-tailed).

The output shows the results of the Pearson correlation coefficient calculation. The results are in the form of a 2×2 matrix of numbers, but all you are interested in is the correlation between the value of cotton production and lynchings in the upper-right corner of the matrix or, what amounts to the same thing, the correlation between lynchings and the value of cotton production in the lower-left corner of the matrix. The correlation between each variable with itself, which is given as 1.000, is about as interesting and informative as $1 \times 1 = 1$. (The correlation of a variable with itself is often assumed to be 1.000, although strictly speaking it is undefined, because if the product-moment formula is used, the calculation involves dividing by zero, but this is a fine point.) If you were studying the correlations between three variables, then the output would show a 3×3 matrix of bivariate correlations, and so on – SPSS can handle very large correlation matrices.

In this case, Pearson's product-moment correlation coefficient is $-.636$ or, as it is usually written, correct to two decimal places, $r = -.64$. The two-tailed significance of this correlation is .000, which does not mean exactly zero but means less than .001 ($p < .001$), and the number of cases is 49 ($N = 49$). Hovland and Sears (1940) got the same result, although they were working before the dawn of the computer age and must have calculated the correlation coefficient by hand.

It is clear that there was a strong and significant negative correlation between the two variables. In line with Hovland and Sears's (1940) hypothesis, as the value of cotton production rose during the period under investigation, the number of lynchings tended to decrease, and as the value of cotton production fell, the number of lynchings tended to rise. In chapter 13 we'll show you how to produce a scatterplot of these data. This is generally a good idea when studying correlations.

5.3 SPEARMAN'S RHO

For convenience, let's calculate Spearman's rho from the data already entered in section 5.2, although Pearson's product-moment correlation coefficient may be more suitable for these scores.

◆ First, get back to the Data Editor window by clicking **Window** in the menu bar near the top of the SPSS Viewer window and then clicking the **SPSS Data Editor** option (review section 4.3 if you've forgotten how to do this).

◆ Click **Statistics** (or **Analyze**) in the menu bar. Click **Correlate** in the drop-down menu, and then click **Bivariate...** in the submenu that appears. The Bivariate Correlations dialog box, which we've already shown you, will open again.

◆ Make sure that the two variables named **cotton** and **lynch** are in the right-hand box, which is labelled **Variables** – if necessary, select them and click the black arrow button to get them into the right-hand box (review section 4.2 if you're unsure).

◆ In the same dialog box, select the type of correlation coefficient you want, in this case **Spearman**. Make sure also that **Pearson** and **Kendall's tau-b** are deselected: if there are ticks in their check boxes, click the boxes to remove the ticks. Select which test of significance you want to be applied to your correlation. **Two-tailed** is the default, but you could have chosen **One-tailed** if you wished by clicking its radio button. To cause correlation coefficients significant at the 0.05 and 0.01 levels to be flagged with a single and a double asterisk, respectively, put a tick in the check box beside **Flag significant correlations**.

◆ If you clicked the **Options...** button, you would open a subdialog box in which you could instruct SPSS to calculate means, standard deviations, cross-product deviations, and covariances, should you require them, and if you had some missing values, you could select a method of dealing with them. The system default for handling missing values is, as before, to exclude cases pairwise.

◆ When you are satisfied that everything in the Bivariate Correlations dialog box is as you want it to be, click the **OK** button, and the SPSS Viewer window will appear, displaying the results. If some of the results scroll off the window, use the scroll bars as explained in section 2.5.

◆ To print a hard copy of the output, follow the procedure described in section 3.2.

➡ Nonparametric Correlations

Correlations

			COTTON	LYNCH
Spearman's rho	COTTON	Correlation Coefficient	1.000	-.637**
		Sig. (2-tailed)	.	.000
		N	49	49
	LYNCH	Correlation Coefficient	-.637**	1.000
		Sig. (2-tailed)	.000	.
		N	49	49

**. Correlation is significant at the .01 level (2-tailed).

The output shows the names of the two variables, namely **cotton** and **lynch**, and three lines of output data: the Spearman rank correlation coefficient ($rs = -.637$), the significance level ($p < .000$), and the number of cases ($N = 49$). Once again, the significance level of .000 should be interpreted as $p < .001$. In this case Spearman's rho is $-.64$ (correct to two decimal places), the significance level is $p < .001$, and the number of cases is 49. These results agree well with those found by using Pearson's product-moment correlation coefficient in section 5.2, and this is to be expected.

◆ If you want to go straight on to the next chapter, click **File** in the menu bar near the top of the SPSS Viewer window, then **New**, then **Data**. If you want to exit from SPSS, click **File** in the menu bar, and then **Exit** at the bottom of the drop-down menu. In either case, when you are prompted, save the data under the filename **lynch.sav**, using the procedure described in section 2.6, if you haven't saved them already, otherwise click **No**.

6 Chi-Square Test

6.1 BACKGROUND

The chi-square statistic is often symbolized by χ^2, the square of *chi*, the 22nd letter of the Greek alphabet. One use of the chi-square test is to determine whether or not two variables measured on nominal or categorical scales, in other words variables that consist of frequencies or counts, are associated with each other. When it is used for this purpose it is called the chi-square test of association, or the chi-square test of independence. Another use is to determine the goodness of fit of a single variable measured on a nominal or categorical scale to a theoretical distribution. This is called the chi-square goodness-of-fit test or the chi-square one-sample test. In either case, the test provides a means of determining whether a set of observed frequencies deviate significantly from a set of expected frequencies. The usual formula for calculating the statistic, called the Pearson chi-square test, is $\chi^2 = \Sigma(O - E)^2/E$, where O represents an observed frequency, E an expected frequency under the null hypothesis, and the summation is over all pairs of observed and expected frequencies. The main alternative is the likelihood ratio chi-square test, which is distributed like chi-square and is computed by doubling the sum of the natural logarithms of the ratios of observed to expected frequencies multiplied by observed frequencies.

For the chi-square test to be valid, the scores must consist of a random sample of data measured on nominal scales, or data from other types of scales reclassified into mutually exclusive categories so that they represent counts or frequencies. The scores must be independent of one another so that, for example, it is not permissible for some scores to come from one respondent or research subject and some other scores from another. When the data are displayed in a contingency table larger than 2×2, none of the expected frequencies in the cells should be less than 1 and no more than 20 per cent should be less than 5. You will be warned by SPSS through a message in the output if these last assumptions are violated. For 2×2 contingency tables with small expected frequencies, SPSS uses Fisher's exact probability test, which does not require large expected frequencies in order to be valid.

6.2 CHI-SQUARE TEST OF ASSOCIATION

The results of a study of 554 people in Los Angeles who tried to give up cigarette smoking by themselves were reported in an article by Cohen et al. (1989). The researchers compared light smokers who smoked 20 or fewer cigarettes (one packet or less) per day with heavy smokers who smoked more than 20 cigarettes per day. After 12 months, the numbers of participants who were still abstaining and the numbers who had relapsed were as shown in the following contingency table of observed frequencies.

	Abstaining	Relapsed
Light smokers	45	285
Heavy smokers	14	210

The researchers analysed these data by using the chi-square test of association, and you are going to check their results. It is clear that 45 of the 330 light smokers (13 per cent) were still abstaining after 12 months, whereas only 14 of the 224 heavy smokers (6 per cent) were still abstaining after 12 months. But is this difference statistically significant? Note that we could have asked the same question the other way round: 45 of the 59 abstainers (76 per cent) were light smokers, whereas only 285 of the 495 relapsers (58 per cent) were light smokers, but is this difference significant? Whichever way the question is asked, it amounts to the same thing: is there a significant association in these results between light versus heavy smoking on the one hand and continuing abstinence versus relapse after 12 months on the other?

This is one of the cases we warned you about at the beginning of section 4.3 in which the data must be entered in a single column of the Data Editor, with grouping variables in separate columns to show (in this case) whether each score refers to light or heavy smokers and whether it refers to abstaining or relapsed smokers. You can't enter the scores as they are set out in the table above; instead you should enter them as shown in Table 6.1.

Table 6.1 Smoking data input format

smoking	status	count
1	1	45
1	2	285
2	1	14
2	2	210

The first column is a grouping variable showing whether the scores refer to participants who were light (1) or heavy (2) smokers at the start of the study. The second column is a grouping variable showing whether the scores refer to participants whose status at the 12-month follow-up was abstaining (1) or relapsed (2). We could just as well have used the value label of 2 for light smokers and 1 for heavy smokers, or 2 for those who remained abstinent and 1 for those who relapsed, or we could have used other numbers: the choice of values for a grouping variable is arbitrary and does not affect the results of the analysis. The third column, of course, contains the actual scores – the frequency counts shown in the earlier table. This table is merely another way of displaying the same data using grouping variables. Now let us show you how to prepare for data input.

6.3 NAMING VARIABLES AND LABELLING VALUES

First, the variables must be named and the values of the grouping variables properly labelled.

◆ In the Data Editor window, double-click the **var** at the top of the first column, and the Define Variable dialog box will open.

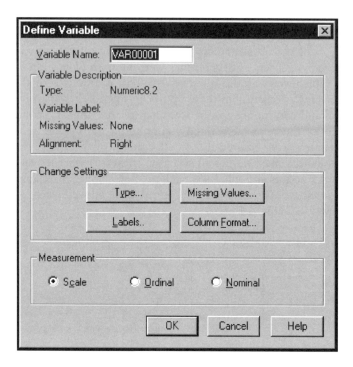

◆ In the Define Variable dialog box, the text box labelled **Variable Name** shows the default name of the first variable: VAR00001. To rename it, just type **smoking** in the text box.
◆ Now define the value labels 1 and 2 of this variable. In the same Define Variable dialog box, click **Labels...**, and the Define Labels subdialog box will open. Go to the part of the box devoted to Value Labels, click inside the text box labelled **Value** and type the numeral **1**. Click inside the text box labelled **Value Label** and type **light**. Click the **Add** button. Repeat the process to define the value 2: click in the text box labelled **Value** and type the numeral **2**, then click in the text box labelled **Value Label** and type **heavy** and click **Add**. Click the button labelled **Continue**.
◆ You will find yourself back in the Define Variable dialog box. Click the **OK** button, and you will be returned to the Data Editor with the first column relabelled.
◆ Repeat the process to rename the second variable and to define its labels. In the Data Editor window, double-click the **var** at the top of the second column, and the Define Variable dialog box will open.
◆ In the Define Variable dialog box, the text box labelled Variable Name shows the default name of the second variable. To rename it, just type **status** in the **Variable Name** text box.

◆ Now define the value labels. Click **Labels...**, and the Define Labels subdialog box will open. Click in the text box labelled **Value** and type the numeral **1**. Click in the text box labelled **Value Label** and type `abstain`. Click the **Add** button. Repeat the process to define the value 2: click in the text box labelled **Value** and type the numeral **2**, then click in the text box labelled **Value Label** and type `relapse` and click **Add**. Click **Continue**.

◆ Back in the Define Variable dialog box, click **OK**, and you will be returned to the Data Editor with the second column relabelled.

◆ Next rename the third variable. In the Data Editor window, double-click the **var** at the top of the third column, and the Define Variable dialog box will open.

◆ In the Define Variable dialog box, the text box labelled **Variable Name** will show the default name of the third variable. To rename it, type `count` in the text box. Because this is not a grouping variable, you don't have to define value labels. The values of this variable are the actual scores. Click **OK**, and you will be returned to the Data Editor, with the third column duly relabelled.

6.4 DATA INPUT AND ANALYSIS

You are now ready to key in the data and initiate the computation.

◆ Key in the data in the format shown in Table 6.1, following the procedure described in section 2.4.

◆ Now you have to tell SPSS which variable contains the frequency scores. The way you do it is rather strange, and you'd never guess it without being told. The official *SPSS for Windows Base System User's Guide* (Norušis, 1993) doesn't even mention it in its section on the chi-square test (pp. 389–92), and people often get stuck at this point. Click **Data** in the menu bar near the top of the Data Editor window, and choose the command **Weight Cases...** at the bottom of the drop-down menu. The Weight Cases dialog box will open.

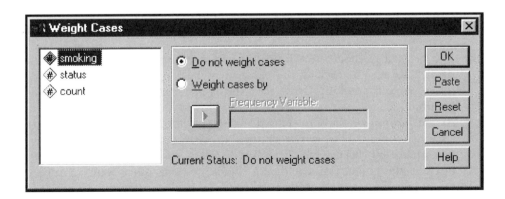

◆ Click the radio button labelled **Weight cases by**. Click the variable called **count** on the left, if it isn't already highlighted, and then click the black arrow button to move it into the text box labelled **Frequency Variable**. Click **OK**. Now you are ready to initiate the computation, but first save the input data.

◆ Save the data on disk for future reference by following the procedure described in section 2.6. Call the file **smoking.sav**.

◆ Click **Statistics** (or **Analyze**) in the menu bar near the top of the Data Editor window, then **Summarize** (or **Descriptive Statistics**), then **Crosstabs...**, and try to remember that this is where the chi-square test of association is hidden. People often struggle to find it.

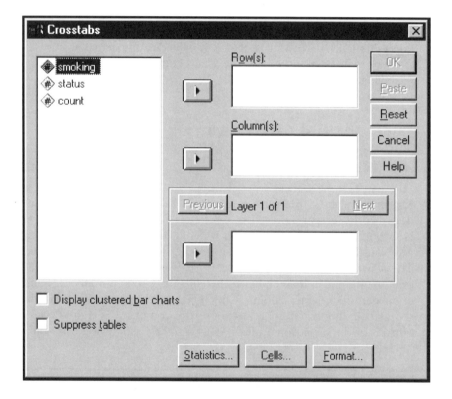

◆ The Crosstabs dialog box will open. Click **smoking** and move it to the box labelled **Row(s)** by clicking the black arrow button. This tells SPSS that the row variable is **smoking**. Now click **status** and move it to the box labelled **Column(s)**.

◆ At the bottom of the Crosstabs dialog box, click the button labelled **Statistics...**, and a subdialog box entitled Crosstabs: Statistics will open. Select **Chi-square** by clicking the check box beside it so that a tick appears in the box. At this point you could also choose various other statistics suitable for nominal data: the contingency coefficient, phi coefficient, Cramér's *V*, or the (Goodman–Kruskal) lambda, which are all chi-square-based measures of association for categorical data, or the uncertainty coefficient, which is a measure of how much information about one variable is provided by the other, and various nonparametric correlations and other procedures are also available.

◆ Click the button labelled **Continue**. When you are returned to the Crosstabs dialog box, click **Cells...**, and a new subdialog box called Crosstabs: Cell Display will open. Here you can customize the output to suit your needs. To display both observed and expected frequencies, which will make inter-pretation of the results easier, ensure that both **Observed** and **Expected** are selected by clicking in the check boxes beside them so that ticks appear there. You could also, if you wished, select percentages (row, column, and total), which would display within each cell the percentage of the cell frequency relative to the row, column and/or total frequency, and you could also select residuals (unstandardized, standardized, and adjusted standardized), which would display differences between observed and expected frequencies. You don't have to select any of these to get the row and column totals of the contingency table itself; these will be displayed anyway. Click **Continue**, and when you are returned to the Crosstabs dialog box, click **OK**.

◆ The SPSS Viewer window will appear with the results of the chi-square analysis displayed. If some of the results scroll off the window, use the scroll bars as explained in section 2.5.

◆ To print a hard copy of the output, follow the procedure described in section 3.2.

➡ Crosstabs

Case Processing Summary

	Cases					
	Valid		Missing		Total	
	N	Percent	N	Percent	N	Percent
SMOKING * STATUS	554	100.0%	0	.0%	554	100.0%

SMOKING * STATUS Crosstabulation

			STATUS		
			abstain	relapse	Total
SMOKING	light	Count	45	285	330
		Expected Count	35.1	294.9	330.0
	heavy	Count	14	210	224
		Expected Count	23.9	200.1	224.0
Total		Count	59	495	554
		Expected Count	59.0	495.0	554.0

Chi-Square Tests

	Value	df	Asymp. Sig. (2-sided)	Exact Sig. (2-sided)	Exact Sig. (1-sided)
Pearson Chi-Square	7.650[b]	1	.006		
Continuity Correction[a]	6.894	1	.009		
Likelihood Ratio	8.136	1	.004		
Fisher's Exact Test				.007	.004
Linear-by-Linear Association	7.636	1	.006		
N of Valid Cases	554				

a. Computed only for a 2x2 table

b. 0 cells (.0%) have expected count less than 5. The minimum expected count is 23.86.

The output includes, first, a summary of the input data, showing that there were no missing data in this case. Second, there is a contingency table showing both the observed frequencies (the input data) and the expected frequencies (based on an assumption of no association between the two variables), together with the row and column totals (often called marginals). This second table is properly labelled with the variable names and value labels that you assigned. The third table includes among other things the following information: the value of chi-square, the degrees of freedom, and the asymptotic (approximated) two-tailed significance level for both Pearson's chi-square and the likelihood ratio chi-square test, and (because this was a 2 × 2 analysis) the two-tailed and one-tailed significance levels calculated from Fisher's exact probability test. Also shown in this third table, labelled Continuity Correction, is the chi-square value, degrees of freedom, and two-tailed significance level for Pearson's chi-square test with a (Yates) correction for continuity, which some statisticians recommend for use with 2 × 2 contingency tables.

The value of Pearson's chi-square, with one degree of freedom, is shown to be 7.650, with a two-tailed significance level of $p < .006$. In the article from which the data were taken (Cohen et al., 1989), Pearson's chi-square was reported as $\chi^2(1) = 7.65$, $p < .01$ (two-tailed), and these results agree perfectly with ours. The two variables are significantly associated with each other. The authors concluded that "heavy smoking self-quitters are less successful at long-term quitting than their light smoking counterparts" (p. 1363).

6.5 CHI-SQUARE GOODNESS-OF-FIT TEST

When a chi-square test is used to compare an observed distribution of frequencies on a single variable with a distribution that is expected on theoretical grounds, it is called a chi-square goodness-of-fit test or a chi-square one-sample test. The method of computing it is essentially the same as for a chi-square test of association, but the

Table 6.2 Bombs falling on London

Number of hits	0	1	2	3	4	5+
Sectors observed	229	211	93	35	7	1
Sectors expected	227	211	98	31	7	2

expected frequencies are supplied by the analyst rather than being estimated from the observed frequencies, and the procedure for computing the results in SPSS is quite different.

Feller (1968, pp. 160–61) discussed an example arising from the bombing of London during the Second World War. An area of south London was hit by a total of 537 bombs, and most residents believed that the bombs were not falling randomly but were clustering in certain small areas. So strong was this belief that many people abandoned their homes after their neighbourhoods had been hit by bombs. If south London is divided into 576 sectors or neighbourhoods of just one square kilometre each, then the numbers of sectors that experienced zero, one, two, three, four, and five or more hits are shown in Table 6.2, together with the theoretical numbers of sectors that would be expected to experience the corresponding numbers of hits according to the Poisson probability distribution if the bombs fell completely at random.

The observed and expected distributions look remarkably similar, which suggests that the belief of wartime Londoners that the bombs clustered in certain neighbourhoods was merely an illusion or a superstition. To establish objectively whether the two distributions are significantly different, you should perform a chi-square goodness-of-fit test by carrying out the following steps:

◆ If you still have data from the previous analysis in the Data Editor, click **File** in the menu bar near the top of the Data Editor window, then click **New** in the menu that drops down, and click **Data** in the submenu that appears. If you haven't saved the data currently in the Data Editor, a message will be displayed asking you whether you want to save them, in which case you should click **Yes** and then follow the procedure described in section 2.6 to save the file under the file name **smoking.sav**, otherwise click **No**.

◆ Following the procedure described in section 6.3, rename the first column of the Data Editor **hits**, and label the values of this variable so that the lowest value, namely 0, represents zero hits, and so on: type the **Value 0** and the **Value Label 0 hits**, the **Value 1** and the **Value Label 1 hit**, the **Value 2** and the **Value Label 2 hits**, the **Value 3** and the **Value Label 3 hits**, the **Value 4** and the **Value Label 4 hits**, and the **Value 5** and the **Value Label 5+ hits**. Rename the second column **count**.

◆ Enter the data in the following format:

hits	count
0	229
1	211
2	93
3	35
4	7
5	1

◆ Tell SPSS which variable contains the frequency scores. Click **Data** in the menu bar near the top of the Data Editor window, and choose the command **Weight Cases...** at the bottom of the drop-down menu. In the Weight Cases dialog box that opens, click the button beside **Weight cases by**. Click the variable called **count**, if it isn't already highlighted, and then click the black arrow button to move this variable into the box labelled **Frequency Variable**. Click **OK**.

◆ Save the input data on disk for future reference by following the procedure described in section 2.6. Call the file **bombs.sav**.

◆ Click **Statistics** (or **Analyze**) in the menu bar near the top of the Data Editor window, then **Nonparametric Tests**, then **Chi-Square...**, and the Chi-Square Test dialog box will open.

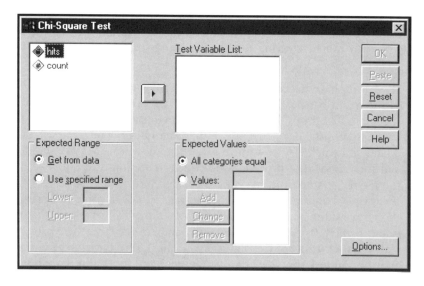

◆ Move the categorical variable hits to the box labelled **Test Variable List**. Select it on the left by clicking it, and transfer it to the **Test Variable List** on the right by clicking the black arrow button.

◆ If the expected frequencies were all equal, you could at this stage use the default **All categories equal**. But in this case the expected frequencies vary from one category to another, and you haven't entered them yet. Click the radio button labelled **Values** and type the expected frequency for category 0, namely **227**, into the text box beside it. Click the **Add** button, which will have lit up. Now type in the expected frequency for category 1, namely **211**, click the **Add** button, and continue in the same way with the rest of the expected frequencies. SPSS assumes that the first expected frequency that you enter is associated with the first value of the categorical variable, the second is associated with the second value, and so on.

◆ In the same Chi-Square Test dialog box there is also an **Options...** button that opens a subdialog box where you could ask for descriptive statistics (mean, minimum, maximum, standard deviation, number of cases, and quartile values of the distribution), and where you could determine how missing values were handled if you had any.

◆ In the Chi-Square Test dialog box, click **OK**, and the SPSS Viewer window will appear with the results of the analysis. If some of the results scroll off the window, use the scroll bars as explained in section 2.5.

HITS

	Observed N	Expected N	Residual
0 = 0 hits	229	227.0	2.0
1 = 1 hit	211	211.0	.0
2 = 2 hits	93	98.0	-5.0
3 = 3 hits	35	31.0	4.0
4 = 4 hits	7	7.0	.0
5 = 5+ hits	1	2.0	-1.0
Total	576		

Test Statistics

	HITS
Chi-Square [a]	1.289
df	5
Asymp. Sig.	.936

a. 1 cells (16.7%) have expected frequencies less than 5. The minimum expected cell frequency is 2.0.

◆ To print a hard copy of the output, follow the procedure described in section 3.2.

The output is quite straightforward and easy to understand. First there is a table labelled **HITS** showing the input data. The first column lists the categories with their labels, the second shows the observed number of hits in each category, the third shows the expected number of hits in each category, and the fourth shows the residuals for each category – the difference between observed and expected frequencies in each category. If the bombs had fallen nonrandomly, then the residuals would have been largest in the categories with either many hits or no hits and smallest in the middle categories. The second table, labelled **Test Statistics**, shows the results of the Chi-square goodness-of-fit test. It shows the value of chi-square to be 1.289, the degrees of freedom (df) 5, and the asymptotic or approximated significance (Asymp. Sig.) .936. (Strictly speaking, you should remove one further degree of freedom that was used for the parameter to calculate the Poisson frequencies, but this isn't a statistics book and we can't go into that.) So the results are $\chi^2(5) = 1.29$, $p = .94$.

This shows that the observed frequencies do not differ significantly from the expected frequencies, which were based on the Poisson probability distribution. If the bombs really did fall at random, and if the bombing were to be repeated many times, a discrepancy as great as this would occur in about 94 per cent of cases. In other words, the observed frequencies were remarkably close to those expected by chance.

◆ If you want to go straight on to the next chapter, click **File** in the menu bar near the top of the SPSS Viewer window, then **New**, then **Data**. If you want to exit from SPSS, then click **File** in the menu bar and then **Exit** (see section 2.7).

7 Independent-Samples and Paired-Samples *T*-Tests

7.1 BACKGROUND

In this chapter we'll describe two versions of a test that is most often used to establish the significance of a difference between the means of two samples of scores. It is calculated by dividing the difference between the means by the standard error of this difference. Its full name is Student's *t*-test, not because students often use it, though they do, but because "Student" was the pen name of the English statistician William Sealy Gosset who developed the theory behind it in 1908 while working for the Guinness brewery in Dublin, though it was later modified by another English statistician called Karl Pearson. Guinness employees were not allowed to publish their research findings, but a special concession was granted to Gosset to publish his work under his pen name.

The independent-samples *t*-test, which we'll describe in section 7.2, is used to test for a significant difference between the means of two independent or unrelated samples of scores. The paired-samples or related-groups or matched-groups *t*-test, described in section 7.3, is used when the two samples of scores are correlated, usually because they represent either pairs of repeated measures from the same individuals or scores from two matched groups. Whenever the paired-samples *t*-test is appropriate, the numbers of scores in the two groups must be equal, because each score in one group is paired with a score in the other, but the independent-samples *t*-test can be used with groups of unequal size. In section 7.4 we'll explain the one-sample *t*-test, which is used to determine whether the mean of a single sample of scores differs significantly from some specified value.

The *t*-test assumes that the scores are measured on at least an interval scale, that they are normally distributed, and (for the standard independent-samples and paired-samples tests) that the variances in the two groups are approximately equal. Many statisticians nowadays consider the *t*-test to be fairly robust against moderate violations of the second and third assumptions, which are called the normality and homogeneity of variance assumptions, at least when equal-sized groups are being compared. But if the scores are measured on only an ordinal scale, or if their distributions are markedly nonnormal or their variances markedly unequal, then the equivalent nonparametric tests described in chapter 8, which are only slightly less powerful than the *t*-test, are sometimes preferred.

7.2 INDEPENDENT-SAMPLES *T*-TEST

An experiment was reported by Fazio, Jackson, Dunton, and Williams (1995) in which an unobtrusive (disguised) measure of racial attitudes was applied to 45 white and 8 black students in the USA. The students, working at computer terminals, were shown a series of 24 words, half of which were positive in meaning (e.g. *attractive, likeable, wonderful*) and half negative (e.g. *annoying, disgusting, offensive*), and they were asked to decide as quickly as possible, by pressing a key labelled *good* or a key labelled *bad*, to which category of meaning each word belonged. Each word was preceded by a photograph of a white or a black person. It was assumed that for people with strongly negative attitudes towards black people, a black face immediately preceding a positive word would cause interference and slow down their responses. The researchers computed an estimate of each student's attitude towards black people by comparing the effects of black and white faces on response times to the positive and negative words. The scores, on a scale in which negative scores indicate negative attitudes and positive scores positive attitudes towards black people, were as follows:

White students: −9, −8, −7, −6, −6, −6, −6, −5, −5, −5, −5, −4, −4, −4, −4, −4, −4, −4, −3, −3, −3, −3, −3, −3, −2, −2, −2, −2, −2, −2, −2, −1, −1, −1, −1, −1, 0, 0, 0, 0, 0, 1, 2, 2, 2
Black students: 0, 1, 1, 2, 2, 3, 6, 7

The scores of the white students look generally lower than those of the black students, but are they *significantly* lower, on average, or could the difference be attributed to chance, given such a small sample of black students? An objective answer to this question will be provided by the results of an independent-samples *t*-test.

Your first task, as always, is to key the data into the Data Editor. You must put all the scores into a single column of the Data Editor, with a grouping variable in another column indicating which group each score belongs to.

◆ In the Data Editor window, double-click **var** at the top of the first column, and the Define Variable dialog box will open.

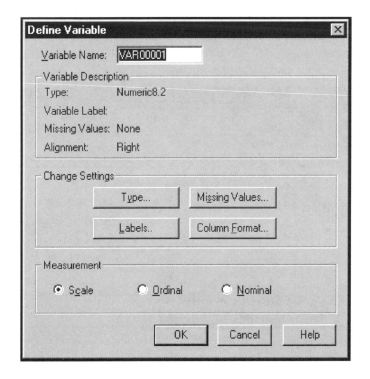

◆ In the Define Variable dialog box, the text box labelled **Variable Name** shows the default name of the first variable: VAR00001. To rename it, type **group** in the text box.

◆ Now define value labels 1 and 2 for this variable. In the same Define Variable dialog box, click **Labels...**, and the Define Labels subdialog box will open. Click inside the text box labelled **Value** and type the numeral **1**. Click inside the text box labelled **Value Label** and type **white**. Click the **Add** button. Repeat the process to define the value 2: in the text box labelled **Value** type the numeral **2**, then click in the text box labelled **Value Label** and type **black**, then click **Add**. Click the button labelled **Continue**.

◆ You'll find yourself back in the Define Variable dialog box. Click **OK**, and you will be returned to the Data Editor, with the first column relabelled.

◆ Next, rename the second variable. In the Data Editor, double-click **var** at the top of the second column, and the Define Variable dialog box will open.

◆ In the Define Variable dialog box, the text box labelled **Variable Name** shows the default name of the second variable. To rename it, type **attitude** in the **Variable Name** text box. Because this is not a grouping variable, you don't have to define value labels. The values of this variable are the actual scores. Click **OK**, and you'll be returned to the Data Editor, with the second column relabelled.

◆ Key the values of the grouping variable into the first column of the Data Editor following the procedure described in section 2.4: type the numeral **1** in the first 45 rows and the numeral **2** in the next 8 rows. Then key the attitude scores in the second column, starting with the 45 scores of the white students and ending with the 8 scores of the black students.

◆ Save the data on disk for future reference by following the procedure described in section 2.6. Call the file **fazio.sav**.

◆ Click **Statistics** (or **Analyze**) in the menu bar near the top of the Data Editor window, then click **Compare Means**.

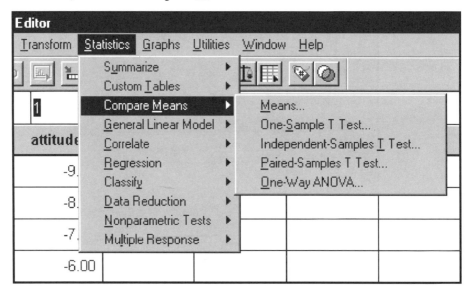

◆ In the **Compare** **M**eans submenu, click **Independent-Samples** **T** **Test...**, and the Independent-Samples T Test dialog box will open.

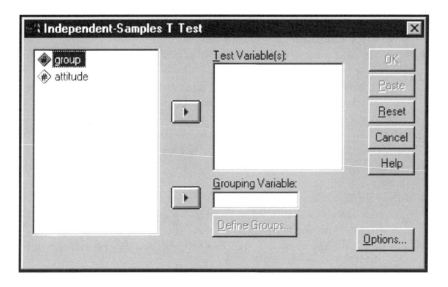

◆ You need to move the variable **attitude** on the left to the box labelled **Test** **Variable(s)** and the variable **group** to the box labelled **Grouping Variable**. Select **attitude** by clicking it, and transfer it to the **Test Variable(s)** box on the right by clicking the upper arrow button. Click **group** on the left, and transfer it to the **Grouping Variable** box with the lower arrow button.

◆ When the variable **group** reappears in the **Grouping Variable** box, it will have acquired a pair of question marks in brackets after its name: **group[? ?]**. The question marks indicate ignorance and concern on the part of SPSS as to which groups the labels **1** and **2** refer to. Click **Define Groups...**, and the Define Groups subdialog box will open.

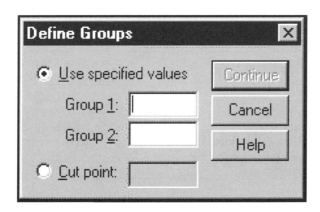

◆ In the text box marked **Group 1** type **1**, then click in the text box marked **Group 2** and type **2**. Only numerical values can be entered in these text boxes: they are values of the grouping variable used to classify the data in the Data Editor window. If you had used different numbers to label the two groups in the Data Editor, then you would have had to enter those numbers here. Click **Continue**, which will have lit up.

◆ You will find yourself back in the Independent-Samples T Test dialog box. There is a button marked **Options...**, which opens a subdialog box where you could change the confidence interval that will be supplied with the output (the system default is the usual 95 per cent confidence interval). In this subdialog box you could also determine how SPSS deals with missing data, if you had any. The system default is to exclude missing data analysis-by-analysis if you perform several *t*-tests, in other words to use all the available data for each separate analysis. For the vast majority of *t*-tests, you wouldn't want to alter these defaults.

◆ In the Independent-Samples T Test dialog box, click **OK**, and the results of the analysis will be displayed in the SPSS Viewer. If some of the data scroll off the window, use the scroll bars to view them (see section 2.5).

◆ To print a hard copy of the output, follow the procedure described in section 3.2.

T-Test

Group Statistics

	GROUP	N	Mean	Std. Deviation	Std. Error Mean
ATTITUDE	white	45	-2.800	2.5990	.3874
	black	8	2.75	2.4928	.8814

Independent Samples Test

		Levene's test for Equality of Variances	
		F	Sig.
ATTITUDE	Equal variances assumed	.061	.806
	Equal variances not assumed		

Independent Samples Test

		t-test for Equality of Means			
		t	df	Sig. (2-tailed)	Mean Difference
ATTITUDE	Equal variances assumed	-5.596	51	.000	-5.5500
	Equal variances not assumed	-5.755	9.908	.000	-5.5500

Independent Samples Test

		t-test for Equality of Means		
			95% Confidence Interval of the Difference	
		Std. Error Difference	Lower	Upper
ATTITUDE	Equal variances assumed	.9917	-7.5410	-3.5590
	Equal variances not assumed	.9627	-7.6978	-3.4022

The output is not difficult to understand. The first table provides some descriptive statistics for the variable labelled ATTITUDE: the number of cases, mean, standard deviation (Std. Deviation), and standard error of the mean (Std. Error Mean) for the white and black groups separately. The second table (which is shown split into three above) provides the *t*-test results, first with the assumption of equal variances (homogeneity of variance), using a pooled variance estimate, and below that without the assumption of equal variances, using separate variance estimates. The results of Levene's test for equality of variances are given to help you decide whether the assumption of equal variances holds. As you can see, the result is non-significant ($F = .061$, $p = .806$), which indicates that the variances of the two groups are not significantly different, so the homogeneity of variance assumption wasn't violated.

With equal variances assumed, $t = -5.596$ (the minus sign is immaterial, reflecting merely the order of the two means in the numerator of the formula used to calculate *t*, so its value may be given as 5.596 or 5.60), the degrees of freedom (df) are 51, and the two-tailed significance level is .000, which does not mean that it is exactly zero but merely that it is less than .001. The second line of the second table gives the same results using separate variance estimates, which might be of interest if the variances were markedly different. Lastly, the right-hand part of the table shows, for both types of analysis, the mean difference (−5.5500), the standard error of the difference, and the lower and upper 95 per cent confidence bounds of the difference.

The results of the analysis are usually written as follows: $t(51) = 5.60$, $p < .001$, two-tailed. The means are significantly different and cannot be attributed to chance. Looking at the means in the first table, it is clear that, even on the unobtrusive or disguised measure of attitudes towards black people used in this research, black students showed significantly more positive attitudes than white students.

If you haven't yet saved the input data in the Data Editor window, we recommend that you save them at this stage so that you don't have to key them in again when we re-analyse them in section 8.2. We suggested that you name the file `fazio.sav`. If you've forgotten how to save data, review section 2.6.

7.3 PAIRED-SAMPLES *T*-TEST

Knox, Morgan, and Hilgard (1974) reported an experiment in which eight university students who had been selected for high hypnotic susceptibility were exposed to pain in hypnosis under two conditions: with suggestions from the hypnotist designed to induce anaesthesia, and without any anaesthesia suggestions. The order of the treatment conditions with and without anaesthesia was counterbalanced – half the students took part in the session without anaesthesia on one day and the session with anaesthesia on the following day, and the other half experienced the anaesthesia and no-anaesthesia conditions in the reverse order. Pain was induced by the method of ischaemia. A tourniquet was applied to each student's arm just above the elbow to obstruct the flow of blood, and the student was instructed to squeeze a hand-exercising device in a controlled manner for 80 seconds and then to relax. When ischaemic pain is induced in this way without hypnosis, the pain begins to mount as soon as the person stops exercising and becomes extremely intense after about eight minutes. In the experiment, the students rated the intensity of the pain on a scale in which zero indicated "no pain sensation", 10 "a very strong sensation of pain", and numbers above 10 even more intense pain sensations. The students' ratings at eight minutes of ischaemia were as shown in Table 7.1.

The ratings of pain without hypnotic anaesthesia look higher than those with hypnotic anaesthesia, but is the difference statistically significant, or could it be

Table 7.1 Hypnotic anaesthesia

Subject	No anaesthesia	Anaesthesia
1	5	1
2	11	0
3	18	0
4	11	2
5	9	2
6	9	2
7	5	1
8	11.5	0

attributed to chance in such a small sample? You can discover the answer with the paired-samples *t*-test as follows:

◆ First get back to the Data Editor by clicking **Window** in the menu bar near the top of the Viewer window and clicking **SPSS Data Editor** in the drop-down menu. If the data from the previous analysis are still there, then click **File** in the menu bar near the top of the window, in the menu that drops down click **New**, and in the submenu that drops down click **Data**. If you haven't saved the previous data, save them under the file name **fazio.sav** when prompted.

◆ Rename the first two columns of the Data Editor. Double-click **var** at the top of the first column, and the Define Variable dialog box will open. The text box labelled **Variable Name** shows the default name of the first variable: VAR00001. To rename it, type **nohypan** in the **Variable Name** text box. Click the **OK** button, and you will be returned to the Data Editor, with the first column relabelled. Repeat the procedure to name the second column **hypan**.

◆ Key the data into the first two columns of the Data Editor (see section 2.4), with scores from the no hypnotic anaesthesia condition in the first column and scores from the hypnotic anaesthesia condition in the second column.

◆ Save the data on disk for future reference by following the procedure described in section 2.6. Call the file **knox.sav**.

◆ Click **Statistics** (or **Analyze**) in the menu bar near the top of the Data Editor window, then click **Compare Means**.

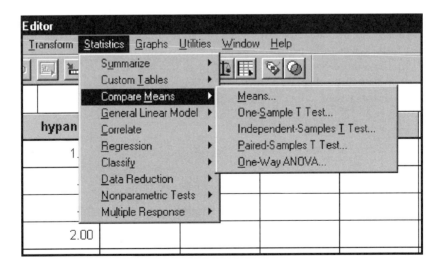

◆ In the submenu that drops down, click **Paired-Samples T Test...**, and the Paired-Samples T Test dialog box will open.

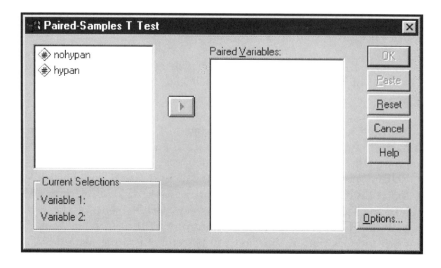

- ◆ You must move both variables on the left to the **Paired Variables** box on the right. Click the variable names **nohypan** and **hypan** separately, so that they appear in the Current Selections list at the bottom as **Variable 1: nohypan** and **Variable 2: hypan,** respectively. Then click the black arrow button and the pair of variables will leap together into the **Paired Variables** box.
- ◆ There is a button marked **Options...** that opens a subdialog box in which you could alter the confidence interval for the difference between the means from the usual default of 95 per cent. In the same dialog box you could also determine the treatment of missing values – the system default is to exclude missing data analysis by analysis if you perform several *t*-tests, in other words to use all available data for each separate analysis. For the vast majority of *t*-tests, you would not need to alter these defaults.
- ◆ In the Paired-Samples T Test dialog box, click **OK**, and the results of the analysis will be displayed in the SPSS Viewer window.
- ◆ To print a hard copy of the output, follow the procedure described in section 3.2. To print only a selection of the output, use the procedure described in section 3.3.

T-Test

Paired Samples Statistics

	GROUP	Mean	N	Std. Deviation	Std. Error Mean
Pair 1	NOHYPAN	9.9375	8	4.1442	1.4652
	HYPAN	1.0000	8	.9258	.3273

Paired Samples Correlations

	N	Correlation	Sig.
Pair 1 NOHYPAN & HYPAN	8	-.428	.290

Paired Samples Test

	Paired Differences					
				95% Confidence Interval of the Difference		
	Mean	Std. Deviation	Std. Error Mean	Lower	Upper	t
Pair 1 NOHYPAN & HYPAN	8.9375	4.6170	1.6324	5.0776	12.7974	5.475

Paired Samples Test

	df	Sig. (2-tailed)
Pair 1 NOHYPAN & HYPAN	7	.001

The first table provides some descriptive statistics. For the NOHYPAN (no hypnotic anaesthesia) and HYPAN (hypnotic anaesthesia) groups separately, it shows the mean, number of scores (N), standard deviation, and standard error of the mean. The second table shows the number of pairs (N), the correlation between the two groups, and the significance of the correlation (Sig.). The third table (split into two above) shows the mean, standard deviation, standard error of the mean, and 95 per cent confidence interval of the paired difference, the value of *t*, the degrees of freedom (df), and the two-tailed significance level.

The value of *t* is shown to be 5.475, with degrees of freedom 7 and two-tailed significance level .001. The results would usually be presented as $t(7) = 5.48$, $p < .001$, two-tailed. These figures agree exactly with those given in the original article by Knox, Morgan, and Hilgard (1974), who concluded, in part, that "for highly hypnotizable subjects, suggested anaesthesia is successful, leading in some cases to the complete elimination of pain and suffering, and averaging, in this experiment, pain and suffering reduction of about 90 per cent" (p. 846).

If you haven't done so already, save the input data in the Data Editor window (see section 2.6) so that you don't have to key the scores in again when we re-analyse them in section 8.3. We suggested that you call the file **knox.sav**. Keep the data in the Data Editor for now; we'll re-use them in the one-sample *t*-test that follows.

7.4 ONE-SAMPLE *T*-TEST

This *t*-test is occasionally used to determine the significance of the difference between the mean of a sample of scores and some specified value. This test can be used, for example, to determine whether the mean of a sample of IQ scores is significantly different from 100, which is average by definition. To save time and trouble we'll illustrate the technique with data from the previous section (7.3). Suppose you want to determine whether the mean of the students' pain ratings under hypnotic anaesthesia was significantly different from zero.

◆ First get back to the Data Editor by clicking **Window** in the menu bar near the top of the Viewer window. Click the **SPSS Data Editor** in the drop-down menu.
◆ If the data from the hypnosis experiment are no longer in the Data Editor, then load the **knox.sav** file from disk using the procedure described in section 3.1. If you haven't got the data on disk either, then key them in by hand (see section 2.4).
◆ Click **Statistics** (or **Analyze**) in the menu bar near the top of the Data Editor window, then **Compare Means**, then **One-Sample T Test...**, and the One-Sample T Test dialog box will open.

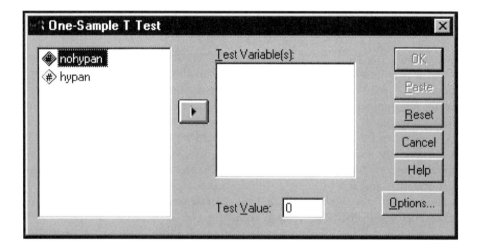

◆ Select the variable **hypan** (the hypnotic group of scores) on the left by clicking it, and transfer it to the box labelled **Test Variable(s)** by clicking the black arrow button.
◆ Make sure that the **Test Value** text box below is showing zero. If you were comparing the mean with some value other than zero, then you would have to enter the specified value into the text box.
◆ There is an **Options...** button that opens a subdialog box in which you could, if you wished, alter the confidence interval to be displayed in the output. You

could also change the method of handling missing data, if you had any, from the default of excluding missing values analysis by analysis, that is, using all the available scores for each test.

◆ Click **OK**, and the results will appear in the SPSS Viewer window.

T-Test

One Sample Statistics

	N	Mean	Std. Deviation	Std. Error Mean
HYPAN	8	1.0000	.9258	.3273

One-Sample Test

	Test Value = 0					
					95% Confidence interval of the Difference	
	t	df	Sig. (2-tailed)	Mean Difference	Lower	Upper
HYPAN	3.055	7	.018	1.000	.2260	1.7740

The first table shows the number of scores (8), the mean (1.0000), the standard deviation (.9258), and the standard error of the mean (.3273). The second table shows that the value of *t* is 3.055, the degrees of freedom (df) 7, the two-tailed significance .018, the mean difference from the specified value 1.0000, and the lower and upper 95 per cent confidence bounds of the difference .2260 and 1.7740, respectively. The results are usually presented as follows: $t(7) = 3.06$, $p < .02$. They show that the hypnotically anaesthetized subjects in the experiment reported by Knox, Morgan, and Hilgard (1974) gave pain ratings that were significantly different from (higher than) zero.

◆ If you want to go straight on to the next chapter, click **File** in the menu bar, then **New**, then **Data**. If you haven't saved the input data, then save them under the file name **knox.sav** when you are prompted. If you want to exit from SPSS at this point, click **File** in the menu bar near the top of the SPSS Viewer window, and then **Exit** at the bottom of the menu that drops down.

8 Mann–Whitney U and Wilcoxon Matched-Pairs Tests

8.1 BACKGROUND

The tests described in this chapter are nonparametric or distribution-free equivalents of the *t*-tests described in chapter 7. The Mann–Whitney *U* test, which we'll describe in section 8.2, is a nonparametric equivalent of the independent-samples *t*-test, and the Wilcoxon matched-pairs test, which we'll describe in section 8.3, is a nonparametric equivalent of the paired-samples *t*-test. They can be used to test the significance of the difference between samples of scores that represent at least ordinal measurement. The Mann–Whitney *U* test, named after the Austrian-born US mathematician Henry Berthold Mann and the US statistician Donald Ransom Whitney who published the test in 1947, involves combining the scores from the two groups, ranking them, and then calculating the statistic *U*, which is the number of times a score from the second group precedes a score from the first group in the ranking. The Wilcoxon matched-pairs test, also called the Wilcoxon signed-ranks test, named after the Irish statistician Frank Wilcoxon who developed the test in 1945, involves calculating the absolute values of the differences between the two variables for each individual or case and then ranking these differences from smallest to largest, and the test statistic *T* is computed from the sums of ranks for negative and positive differences.

8.2 MANN–WHITNEY *U* TEST

To save time, you are going to re-analyse the data from Fazio, Jackson, Dunton, and Williams (1995) that you used in section 7.2. We suggested that you save the data under the file name **fazio.sav**. If you didn't save the file, key the data in again and name the variables as described towards the beginning of that section. If you did, then load the file from disk using the procedure described in section 3.1.

◆ Click on **Statistics** (or **Analyze**) in the menu bar near the top of the Data Editor window, then click **Nonparametric Tests**.

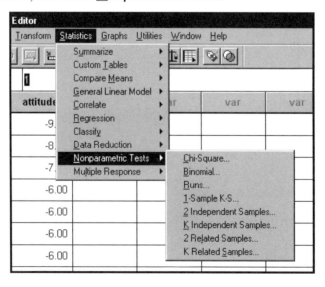

◆ Click **2 Independent Samples...** and the Two-Independent-Samples Tests dialog box will open.

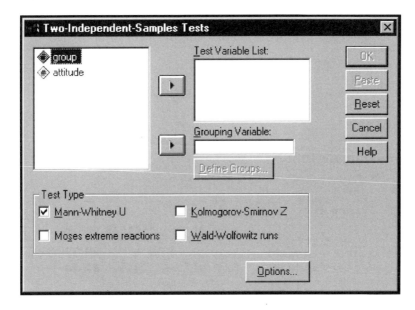

◆ You need to move the variable **attitude** on the left to the box labelled **Test Variable List** and the variable labelled **group** to the box labelled **Grouping Variable**. Select **attitude** by clicking it to highlight it, and transfer it to the **Test Variable List** box on the right by clicking the upper arrow button. Click **group** on the left, and transfer it to the **Grouping Variable** box by clicking the other arrow button.

◆ When the variable **group** reappears in the **Grouping Variable** box, it will have acquired a pair of question marks in brackets after its name: **group[? ?]**. You need to tell SPSS which groups the labels **1** and **2** refer to. Click **Define Groups...** and a subdialog box will open.

◆ In the text box marked **Group 1** type **1**, then click in the text box marked **Group 2** and type **2**. Only numerical values can be entered in these boxes: they are values of the grouping variable used to classify the data in the Data Editor window. Click **Continue**.

◆ In the Two-Independent-Samples Tests dialog box, from the group labelled **Test Type**, choose **Mann-Whitney U** by clicking in the check box beside its name so that a tick appears there if it isn't there already. Make sure that **Kolmogorov-Smirnov Z**, **Moses extreme reactions**, and **Wald-Wolfowitz runs** are all deselected (to remove a tick, just click it). These are alternative nonparametric tests that can be performed on two independent samples of scores.

◆ There is also an **Options...** button that opens a subdialog box in which you could ask for descriptive statistics to be supplied with the output (the mean, minimum, maximum, standard deviation, number of missing cases, and quartile values for each variable), and you could determine how missing values are handled, if you had any (the system default is to exclude them on a test-by-test basis if you run more than one test).

◆ In the Two-Independent-Samples Tests dialog box, click **OK**, and the results will appear in the SPSS Viewer. Use the scroll bars to view them (see section 2.5).

◆ To print a hard copy of the output, follow the procedure described in section 3.2.

Npar Tests

Mann-Whitney Test
Ranks

GROUP		N	Mean Rank	Sum of Ranks
ATTITUDE	white	45	23.37	1051.50
	black	8	47.44	379.5
	Total	53		

Test Statistics[b]

	ATTITUDE
Mann-Whitney U	16.500
Wilcoxon W	1051.500
Z	-4.082
Asymp. Sig. (2-tailed)	.000
Exact Sig. [2*(1-tailed Sig.)]	.000[a]

a. Not corrected for ties.

b. Grouping Variable: GROUP

The first table shows the mean rank and sum of ranks of the 45 white and 8 black participants. The second table gives the value of the Mann–Whitney *U* statistic (16.500) together with the asymptotic (approximated) and exact two-tailed significance levels (both .000, to be interpreted as less than .001). Also included in the second table is the value of the statistic Wilcoxon *W* (the sum of ranks for the first group) and of *Z* (the standardized normal approximation of the test statistic, from which the asymptotic significance level is estimated). The usual style for reporting the results is simply $U(51) = 16.50$, $p < .0001$, two-tailed. These results agree well with those of section 7.2, which is to be expected, because when the Mann–Whitney *U* test is applied to data that are suitable for the independent-samples *t*-test, its power-efficiency is about 95 per cent, even for moderate-sized samples, and approaches 95.5 as sample sizes increase.

◆ Return to the Data Editor by clicking **Window** in the menu bar near the top of the SPSS Viewer window, and then clicking **SPSS Data Editor**.
◆ Click **File** in the menu bar near the top of the Data Editor, then **New**, then **Data**. If you haven't already saved the data from the Fazio experiment, you may wish to save them when prompted under the file name **fazio.sav**.

8.3 WILCOXON MATCHED-PAIRS TEST

Now you are going to re-analyse the data from Knox, Morgan, and Hilgard (1974), discussed in section 7.3, which we advised you to save under the file name **knox.sav**. If you have the file on disk, then load it up using the procedure described in section 3.1. If you don't have a copy of the data, key the scores in again and name the variables as described towards the beginning of section 7.3.

◆ Click **Statistics** (or **Analyze**) in the menu bar near the top of the Data Editor window, then click **Nonparametric Tests**, then **2 Related Samples...** and the Two-Related-Samples Tests dialog box will open.

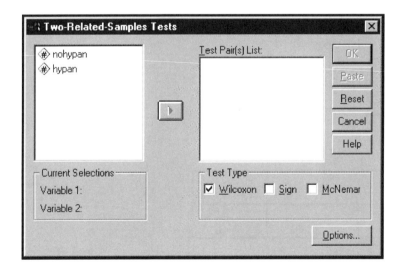

◆ As with the paired-samples *t*-test, you need to move both variables from the left to the **Test Pair(s) List** on the right. Click the variable names **nohypan** and **hypan** separately, so that they appear in the **Current Selections** list at the bottom as **Variable 1: nohypan** and **Variable 2: hypan**, respectively. Then click the black arrow button and the pair of variables will leap together into the **T**est **Pair(s) List**.

◆ Once again, there is an **Options...** button that opens a subdialog box in which you could ask for descriptive statistics to be supplied with the output (the mean, minimum, maximum, standard deviation, and the number of missing cases, and quartile values for each variable), and you could determine how missing values are handled, if you had any (the system default is to exclude them on a test-by-test basis if you run more than one test).

◆ In the Two-Related-Samples Tests dialog box, click **OK**, and the results of the analysis will appear in the SPSS Viewer.

◆ To print a hard copy of the output, follow the procedure described in section 3.2.

NPar Tests

Wilcoxon Signed Ranks Test

Ranks

		N	Mean Rank	Sum of Ranks
HYPAN - NOHYPAN	Negative Ranks	8[a]	4.50	36.00
	Positive Ranks	0[b]	.00	.00
	Ties	0[c]		
	Total	8		

a. HYPAN < NOHYPAN

b. HYPAN > NOHYPAN

c. NOHYPAN = HYPAN

Test Statistics[b]

	HYPAN - NOHYPAN
Z	-2.527[a]
Asymp. Sig. (2-tailed)	.012

a. Based on positive ranks.

b. Wilcoxon Signed Ranks Test

The first table shows the number of negative ranks (the number of times the rank of variable 1 is less than the rank of variable 2), the number of positive ranks (the number of times the rank of variable 1 is greater than the rank of variable 2), and the number of ties (scores with the same rank). The footnotes below the table make the directions of the differences clear. In this experiment, the ranks of scores in the hypnotic anaesthesia group were lower than those in the no hypnotic anaesthesia group in all eight cases, with no ties. The second table shows the value of Z, the standardized normal approximation to the test statistic and the asymptotic two-tailed significance estimated from the normal approximation. The minus sign attached to Z is unimportant, reflecting merely the order in which the groups were compared. Values of Z are associated with exactly the same probability whether they are positive or negative, because the standardized normal distribution is symmetrical about a mean of zero. The results of this analysis would normally be reported as follows: $Z = 2.52$, $p = .01$, two-tailed. The results agree well with those of the paired-samples *t*-test of section 7.3, although at a slightly lower significance level. When the Wilcoxon test is applied to data that are suitable for the paired-samples *t*-test, its power efficiency is about 95 per cent for small samples.

◆ If you want to go straight on to the next chapter, click **File** in the menu bar, then **New**, then **Data**. Otherwise, exit from SPSS by clicking **File** in the menu bar near the top of the SPSS Viewer window, and then **Exit** at the bottom of the menu that drops down. If you have not already saved the input data on disk, you may wish to save them under the file name **knox.sav** when prompted.

9 One-Way Analysis of Variance

9.1 BACKGROUND

One-way analysis of variance (one-way ANOVA) is a statistical procedure for testing the significance of the differences among several independent group means by partitioning the total variance in the dependent variable into effects due to different levels of the independent variable, which in ANOVA is sometimes called the factor, plus error variance. You may find it helpful to think of one-way analysis of variance as a generalization of the independent-samples *t*-test designed to determine the significance of the differences among three or more (rather than just two) group means. Or to put it another way, the independent-samples *t*-test is merely a special case of one-way analysis of variance for determining the significance of the difference between means when there are just two means to compare.

The analysis described in this chapter is based on the assumption that the scores are all statistically independent of one another. If the scores are not independent, usually because they come from repeated measures on the same group of individuals, then the analysis requires a slightly different procedure, which we'll describe in chapter 11.

9.2 DATA INPUT

Corston and Colman (1996) reported the results of an experiment in which female students attempted to use a mouse pointer to track a small square as it moved erratically around a computer screen. The women who participated in the experiment were randomly assigned to three treatment conditions in which they performed the task either alone, in the presence of a female audience, or in the presence of a male audience. The percentages of time on target in the three audience conditions were as shown in Table 9.1.

Table 9.1 Audience effects

	Audience condition		
Subject	*Alone*	*Female*	*Male*
1	31.4	41.0	18.8
2	2.8	46.0	21.8
3	34.8	54.0	26.8
4	27.0	36.4	23.2
5	12.6	50.4	40.8
6	24.4	31.0	12.0
7	18.4	47.2	13.6
8	20.2	51.4	16.0
9	21.0	45.8	35.2
10	20.2	40.0	22.2
11	12.2	45.8	25.4
12	12.2	25.8	2.8

The tracking scores look distinctly higher in the Female audience condition than in the Alone and Male audience conditions, but are the means of the three audience conditions significantly different from one another? Did the manipulation of the independent variable have a significant effect on the tracking scores? One-way ANOVA will answer these questions.

First, the data must be entered into the Data Editor in a single column, with a grouping variable in a separate column to indicate which group each score belongs to. We introduced you to this method of formatting data, which is necessary for many SPSS analyses, in section 4.3. To enter the data, proceed as follows:

◆ Begin by naming the first two columns of the Data Editor **score** and **audience**, respectively. Double-click the **var** at the top of the first column, and the Define Variable dialog box (with which you should by now be familiar) will open. The text box labelled **Variable Name** shows the default name of the first variable: VAR00001. To rename it, type **score** in the **Variable Name** text box. Click the **OK** button, and you will be returned to the Data Editor, with the first column relabelled. Repeat the procedure to name the second column **audience**, but don't click **OK** yet.

◆ Now define value labels 1, 2, and 3 for the variable **audience**. In the same Define Variable dialog box, click **Labels...**, and the familiar Define Labels subdialog box will open. Go to the part of the box devoted to Value Labels, click in the text box labelled **Value** and type the numeral **1**. Click in the text box labelled **Value Label** and type **alone**. Click the **Add** button. Repeat the process to define the value 2: in the text box labelled **Value** type the numeral **2**, then click in the text box labelled **Value Label** and type **female**, then click **Add**. Finally, repeat the process to define the value 3: in the text box labelled **Value** type the numeral **3**, then click in the text box labelled **Value Label** and type **male**, then click **Add**. Click **Continue**, and you will be returned to the Define Variable dialog box.

◆ In the Define Variable dialog box you could also, if you wished, click **Type...** to open a subdialog box in which you could define the data type if your scores were not numeric (which is the default setting); **Missing Values...** to open a subdialog box to decide how to treat missing values, if you had any (the default setting is **No missing values**); or **Column Format...** to open a subdialog box to alter the display of data in the Data Editor, if for example you had scores that required a column width greater than eight characters in the Data Editor. But for most purposes the defaults are quite satisfactory.

◆ Click **OK** in the Define Variable dialog box, and you will be returned to the Data Editor. Now key all the data from the table above into the first two columns of the Data Editor. The scores should be entered in the first 36 rows of the first column and the grouping variable in the second column as follows:

	score	audience
1	31.40	1.00
2	2.80	1.00
3	34.80	1.00
4	27.00	1.00
5	12.60	1.00
6	24.00	1.00

	score	audience
13	41.00	2.00
14	46.00	2.00
15	54.00	2.00
16	36.40	2.00
17	50.40	2.00
18	31.00	2.00

◆ Save the data on disk for future reference by following the procedure described in section 2.6. Call the file **audience.sav**.

9.3 ANALYSIS

The analysis of one-way ANOVA data is quite straightforward.

◆ Click **Statistics** (or **Analyze**) near the top of the Data Editor window, then click **Compare Means**.

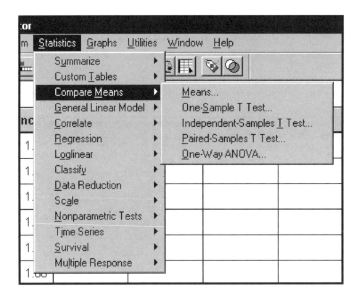

◆ Click **One-Way ANOVA...** and the One-Way ANOVA dialog box will open.

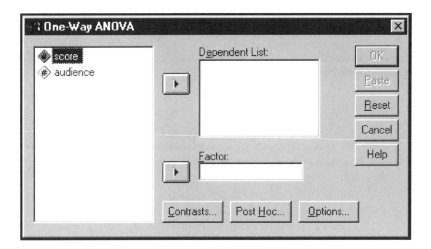

◆ You need to move the variable **score** to the **Dependent List** box and **audience** to the **Factor** box. Click **score** on the left, if it is not already highlighted, then click the upper arrow button pointing to the box labelled **Dependent List** on the right. Then click **audience** on the left, followed by the lower arrow button pointing to the box labelled **Factor**.

◆ If you wished to calculate contrasts – planned *t*-test comparisons of pairs of means – you could at this stage click **Contrasts...** and a subdialog box would open. Then, if for example you wanted a single test to compare the mean of the Alone condition with the other two means, you could instruct SPSS to calculate the contrast 0.5FEMALE + 0.5MALE − 1.0ALONE (the coefficients must sum to zero). This should not be used for *post hoc* or a posteriori multiple comparisons (see immediately below).

♦ Click **Post Hoc...** and the Post Hoc Multiple Comparisons subdialog box will open.

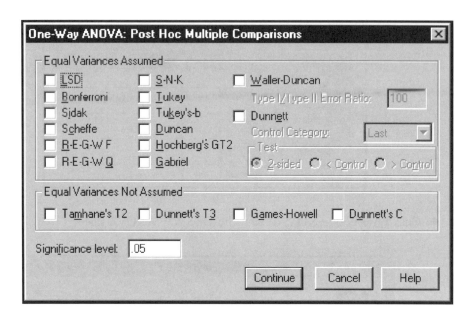

♦ You have a choice of no fewer than 18 different methods of making *post hoc* or a posteriori multiple comparisons between the means. These tests show which means differ from which others if the overall result reveals that there is *some* difference between the three means. The first test listed is **LSD**, the least-significant difference test. It uses pairwise *t*-tests to compare each mean with every other mean but does not make any adjustment for the fact that several comparisons are made using the same data and therefore offers no protection against a Type I error – rejecting the null hypothesis of no effect when it is true. This is so because if three comparisons are made, then even if the data were completely random, the probability that one of them would be significant at $p < .05$ by chance alone would be greater than .05, because there would be three ways rather than one in which this could happen by chance: Mean 1 could be significantly different from Mean 2, Mean 1 from Mean 3, or Mean 2 from Mean 3. **Bonferroni**, the Bonferroni *t*-test, adjusts the significance level crudely and drastically: if three comparisons are made at $p < .05$, it requires a significance level of $.05/3 = .017$ for each separate comparison. The other tests in the group labelled **Equal Variances Assumed** are the most commonly used multiple comparison procedures, each with its own advantages and disadvantages, including **Scheffe** (The Scheffé test), **S-N-K** (the Student–

Newman–Keuls test, also called the Newman–Keuls test), **Tukey** (Tukey's honestly significant difference test or Tukey-HSD test), **Tukey's-b** (Tukey's b test), **Duncan** (Duncan's multiple range test), and **Dunnett** (Dunnett's specialized test for comparing a single control mean with a set of other means). There are further tests in the group labelled **Equal Variances Not Assumed**. We recommend Tukey's honestly significant difference test (the Tukey-HSD test) for most purposes, because it is widely used, and it offers adequate protection against a Type I error without being excessively conservative, as are the Bonferroni t-test and Scheffé's test. Click the check box beside **Tukey** so that a tick appears there, and make sure that the other options are deselected by clicking in their check boxes if there are ticks in them.

◆ In the same Post Hoc Multiple Comparisons subdialog box, you could if you wished change the default significance level of the test from $p < .05$ to some other value by clicking in the text box labelled **Significance level**, deleting .05, and typing in a new value such as .01 or .001. Also, if you had chosen Dunnett's test for comparing a single control mean with a set of other means, you could choose a one-tailed test by clicking a radio button labelled < **Control** to test whether the mean at any level of the factor is smaller than that of the control mean, or > **Control** to test whether the mean at any level of the factor is greater than that of the control mean. The default is a two-tailed test. For the moment we suggest that you ignore these options and click **Continue**.

◆ Back in the One-Way ANOVA dialog box, Click **Options...** and the One-Way ANOVA: Options subdialog box will open.

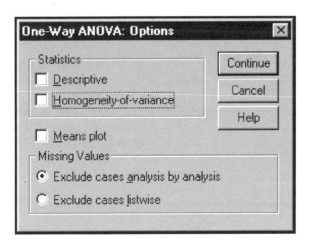

◆ The **Statistics** group in the One-Way ANOVA: Options subdialog box allows you to ask for **Descriptive** statistics, which will cause SPSS to supply the number of cases, mean, standard deviation, standard error, minimum, maximum, and 95 per cent confidence interval of the dependent variable in each group. This information, especially the means, is almost always useful, so click the check box beside **Descriptive** to put a tick there. Click the check box beside **Homogeneity-of-variance** so that SPSS supplies the results of the Levene test, because it is an assumption of one-way ANOVA that the variances of the groups are approximately equal. If you wished, you could also click the check box beside **Means plot** to request a graph showing the means for each group on the dependent variable, and if you had any missing data you could use the radio button to change from the default method of handling missing values. Click **Continue**.

◆ Back in the One-Way ANOVA dialog box click **OK**, and the SPSS Viewer window will appear with the results of the analysis. If some of the results scroll out of sight, use the scroll bars as explained in section 2.5.

◆ To print a hard copy of the output, follow the procedure described in section 3.2. To print only a selection of the output, use the procedure described in section 3.3.

9.4 RESULTS

Oneway

Descriptives

SCORE

	N	Mean	Std. Deviation	Std. Error	95% Confidence Interval for Mean		Minimum	Maximum
					Lower Bound	Upper Bound		
alone	12	19.7667	9.0082	2.6004	14.0431	25.4902	2.80	34.80
female	12	42.9000	8.4473	2.4385	37.5329	48.2671	25.80	54.00
male	12	21.5500	10.2106	2.9475	15.0625	28.0375	2.80	40.80
Total	36	28.0722	13.9396	2.3233	23.3557	32.7887	2.80	54.00

Test of Homogeneity of Variances

SCORE

Levene Statistic	df1	df2	Sig.
.057	2	33	.944

ANOVA

SCORE

	Sum of Squares	df	Mean Square	F	Sig.
Between Groups	3976.616	2	1988.308	23.232	.000
Within Groups	2824.357	33	85.587		
Total	6800.972	35			

Post Hoc Tests

Multiple Comparisons

Dependent Variable: SCORE
Tukey HSD

(I) AUDIENCE	(J) AUDIENCE	Mean Difference (I-J)	Std. Error	Sig.	95% Confidence Interval	
					Lower Bound	Upper Bound
alone	female	-23.1333*	3.777	.000	-32.4009	-13.8658
	male	-1.7833	3.777	.885	-11.0509	7.4842
female	alone	23.1333*	3.777	.000	13.8658	32.4009
	male	21.3500*	3.777	.000	12.0824	30.6176
male	alone	1.7833	3.777	.885	-7.4842	11.0509
	female	-21.3500*	3.777	.000	-30.6176	-12.0824

*. The mean difference is significant at the .05 level.

Homogeneous Subsets

SCORE

Tukey HSD[a]

AUDIENCE	N	Subset for alpha = .05	
		1	2
alone	12	19.7667	
male	12	21.5500	
female	12		42.9000
Sig.		.885	1.000

Means for groups in homogeneous subsets are displayed.
a. Uses Harmonic Mean Sample Size = 12.000.

The first table provides the descriptive statistics that you requested. For each of the three treatment conditions, labelled alone, female, and male, the table shows the number of scores, mean, standard deviation, standard error, lower and upper bounds of the 95 per cent confidence interval, minimum, and maximum, and in the bottom line, labelled Total, these statistics are all supplied for the combined groups. The most important data here are the three means. It is clear that the mean for the Female audience condition (42.9000) is higher than the other two means (19.7667 and 21.5500), but it is not yet clear whether it is significantly higher than both of the other means or higher than the smallest mean only, and there might also be other significant differences among the three means.

The second table supplies the results of the Levene test of homogeneity of variance. The results are nonsignificant (the significance level is not less than .05), showing that there is no reason to believe that the variances of the three groups are different from one another, which would violate the homogeneity of variance assumption of ANOVA and make the results difficult to interpret.

The third table is a standard ANOVA table showing the sum of squares, degrees of freedom (df), and mean square of the between-groups variance and the within-groups variance, the value of F (the between-groups variance divided by the within-groups variance), and the significance (Sig.) of the F ratio. The results show that the three means are significantly different from one another: the significance level of the F ratio is given as 000 (which you should interpret as less than .001). All that the basic one-way ANOVA test establishes is that there is some significant difference among the three means. Multiple comparisons are needed to establish where the differences lie.

The fourth and fifth tables show the results of the Tukey-HSD multiple comparison test in slightly different ways. Both tables show the results of multiple pairwise comparisons among the three groups, representing the three audience conditions: Alone, Male audience, and Female audience. In the fourth table, the first pair of rows in the body of the table shows that the Alone group mean is significantly different from the Female group mean (an asterisk against the mean difference indicates a difference significant at the .05 level) but not from the Male group mean. The second pair of rows shows that the Female group mean is significantly different from the Alone group mean but not from the Male group mean. The third pair of rows shows that the Male group mean is not significantly different from the Alone group mean but is significantly different from the Female group mean. Various descriptive statistics are also listed in this table.

In the fifth and last table, the three groups are divided into what are called homogeneous subsets. The Alone and Male groups are in one homogeneous subset, and the Female group is in another. This means that the means of the Alone and Male groups are not significantly different from each other (in other words they form a homogeneous subset) according to the Tukey-HSD test, at the significance level chosen, but they are both significantly different from the mean of the Female group. As you can see in the same table, the means of the Alone and Male groups are 19.7667 and 21.5500, respectively. These means are quite close together, and they are both much smaller than the mean of the Female group, which is 42.9000.

We may therefore conclude, as Corston and Colman (1996) did, that the audience condition had a significant effect on the performance of women in the computer-based tracking task. The results of the ANOVA are normally written: $F(2, 33) = 23.23$, $p < .001$. *Post hoc* Tukey-HSD tests showed that, in terms of percentage of time on target, the women who performed the task in the presence of a female audience scored significantly higher ($M = 42.90$) than the women who performed the task either alone ($M = 19.77$) or in the presence of a male audience ($M = 21.55$), and that no other differences were statistically significant.

◆ If you want to go straight on to the next chapter, click **File** in the menu bar near the top of the SPSS Viewer window, then **New**, then **Data**. If you want to exit from SPSS, click **File** and then **Exit**.

10 Multifactorial Analysis of Variance

10.1 BACKGROUND

Multifactorial analysis of variance (multifactorial ANOVA) is an extension of one-way ANOVA, which you covered in chapter 9. It is used for analysing the simultaneous effects of two or more independent variables, usually called factors, on a dependent variable. In multifactorial ANOVA, the differences among several group means are analysed by partitioning the total variance in the dependent variable into effects due to each of the factors, called main effects, interactions between the factors, and error variance.

The feature of multifactorial ANOVA that differentiates it from one-way ANOVA is the inclusion of interaction terms in the statistical model. The results of a factorial experiment – one involving two or more independent variables or factors – could, of course, be analysed by applying one-way ANOVA to each factor separately; but this approach is often considered to be an error, partly because it fails to take account of possible interaction effects. Imagine an experiment designed to examine the effects of age (younger versus older) and gender (female versus male) on the performance of children on a spatial reasoning task. Suppose the results showed no significant main effects, in other words no significant difference between the mean scores of the boys and the girls and no significant difference between the mean scores of younger and older children. The interaction between the two factors, gender and age, could nevertheless be significant if, for example, in the younger age group girls performed better than boys (because girls tend to mature earlier than boys) whereas in the older age group boys performed better than girls (because mature males usually outperform mature females at spatial reasoning tasks). In the terminology of multifactorial ANOVA, we would then say that the main effects were not significant but that the Gender × Age interaction was significant. As in this hypothetical example, an interaction effect is written with a multiplication sign between the factors, which are usually written with initial capitals. In factorial experiments with more than two factors, three-way and sometimes even higher-order interactions are possible, but they tend to be difficult to interpret. We'll give you some tips about the interpretation of interactions towards the end of this chapter.

The analysis described in this chapter is based on the assumption that the scores are all statistically independent of one another. If scores across one or more of the factors are not independent, usually because they represent repeated measures taken from the same group of individuals, then you require a slightly different procedure, which we'll describe in chapter 11.

10.2 DATA INPUT

The data that you are going to analyse come from the experiment by Corston and Colman (1996) outlined in section 9.2, which was slightly more complex than we revealed in that section. In fact, it was a factorial experiment with two independent variables: gender (of the subjects or experimental participants) and audience condition. Both men and women students attempted to use a mouse pointer to track a small square as it moved erratically around a computer screen. The men and women who participated in the experiment were randomly assigned to treatment conditions in which they performed the task either alone, in the presence of a female audience, or in the presence of a male audience. There were therefore six treatment conditions in all:

WA: women alone
WFA: women with a female audience
WMA: women with a male audience
MA: males alone
MFA: males with a female audience
MMA: males with a male audience

Twelve women and twelve men were assigned randomly to each of the three audience conditions, and the percentages of time on target were as shown in Table 10.1.

Table 10.1 Gender and audience effects

Subject	WA	WFA	WMA	MA	MFA	MMA
1	31.4	41.0	16.2	28.8	53.2	25.2
2	2.8	46.0	21.8	31.6	48.6	7.4
3	34.8	54.0	26.8	45.4	34.0	15.6
4	27.0	36.4	23.2	37.8	66.2	32.2
5	9.8	50.4	40.8	26.4	47.4	45.6
6	24.4	31.0	12.0	26.8	24.6	45.8
7	18.4	47.2	13.6	31.0	52.4	58.6
8	14.2	51.4	16.0	19.4	39.8	56.4
9	21.0	45.8	35.2	55.6	45.6	47.8
10	20.2	40.0	22.2	72.2	44.4	64.0
11	12.2	45.8	25.4	49.2	52.6	38.4
12	12.2	25.8	2.8	47.0	46.8	55.6

The tracking scores of both women and men look higher in the female audience conditions than in the alone and male audience conditions, but statistical analysis is required to determine whether the differences between the means are statistically significant, and whether the Gender × Audience interaction is statistically significant. Here's how to compute a two-way ANOVA.

The data must be entered into the Data Editor in a single column, with a grouping variable in the second column to indicate whether each score comes from a woman or a man subject and another grouping variable in the third column to indicate which of the three audience conditions it belongs to. We introduced the idea behind grouping variables in section 4.3. Here's how you should enter the data (there are only 72 scores; it won't take you very long).

◆ Begin by naming the first three columns of the Data Editor **score**, **gender**, and **audience**, respectively, and defining the value labels for the last two of these. Double-click the **var** at the top of the first column, and the Define Variable dialog box, with which you should be quite familiar, will open. The text box labelled **Variable Name** shows the default name of the first variable: VAR00001. To rename it, type **score** in the text box. Click the **OK** button, and you will be returned to the Data Editor, with the first column relabelled. Repeat the procedure to name the second column **gender**, but don't click **OK** yet.

◆ First define the value labels 1 and 2 for the variable **gender**. In the same Define Variable dialog box, click **Labels...**, and the Define Labels subdialog box will open. Go to the part devoted to Value Labels, click in the text box labelled **Value** and type the numeral **1**. Click in the text box labelled **Value Label** and type **women**. Click the **Add** button. Repeat the process to define the value 2: in the text box labelled **Value** type the numeral **2**, then click in the text box labelled **Value Label** and type **men**, then click **Add**. You have told SPSS that 1 stands for women and 2 for men. Click **Continue**, and you will be returned to the Define Variable dialog box.

◆ Click **OK** in the Define Variable dialog box, and you'll be returned to the Data Editor. Double-click the **var** at the top of the third column, and the Define Variable dialog box will open again. The text box labelled **Variable Name** shows the default name. To rename it, type **audience** in the text box, and don't click **OK** yet.

◆ Now define value labels 1, 2, and 3 for the variable **audience**. In the same Define Variable dialog box, click **Labels...**, and the Define Labels subdialog box will open. Go to the part devoted to Value Labels, click in the text box labelled **Value** and type the numeral **1**. Click in the text box labelled **Value Label** and type **alone**. Click the **Add** button. Repeat the process to define the value 2: in the text box labelled **Value** type the numeral **2**, then click in the text box labelled **Value Label** and type **female**, followed by **Add**. Finally, repeat the process to define the value 3: in the text box labelled **Value** type the numeral **3**, then click in the text box labelled **Value Label** and type **male**, then click **Add**. Click **Continue**, and you will be returned to the Define Variable dialog box.

◆ In the Define Variable dialog box you could also, if you wished, click **Type...** to open a subdialog box in which you could define the type of data if they were not ordinary numeric scores (which is the default); you could also click **Missing Values...** to open a subdialog box to inform SPSS about missing values, if you had any (the default setting is **No missing values**); or you could click **Column Format...** to open a subdialog box to alter the display of data in the Data Editor, if for example you had scores that required a column width greater than eight characters in the Data Editor. But for most purposes the defaults are quite satisfactory, and these dialog boxes seldom need to be opened.

◆ Click **OK** in the Define Variable dialog box, and you will be returned to the Data Editor. Now key the data from Table 10.1 into the first three columns of the Data Editor. The data should be set out as follows:

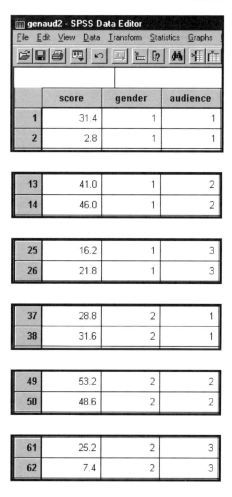

◆ Save the data on disk for future reference by following the procedure described in section 2.6. Call the file **genaud.sav**.

10.3 ANALYSIS

The procedure for analysing the data is not difficult, especially now that you are familiar with the general principles.

◆ Click **Statistics** (or **Analyze**) in the menu bar near the top of the Data Editor. In the drop-down menu that appears, click **General Linear Model**.

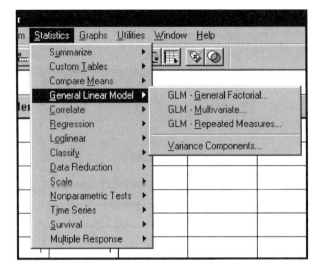

◆ Click **GLM – General Factorial...** (or **Univariate...**) and the GLM – General Factorial (or Univariate) dialog box will open.

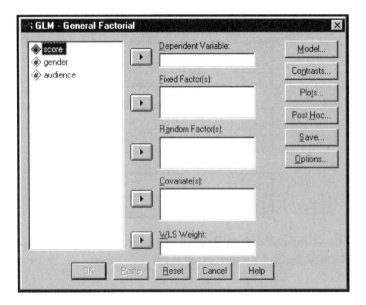

◆ In the GLM – General Factorial (or Univariate) dialog box, you have to tell SPSS that **score** is the dependent variable and that **gender** and **audience** are factors. Click **score** on the left and move it to the box labelled **Dependent Variable** by clicking the top arrow button. Then click **gender** on the left and move it to the box labelled **Fixed Factor(s)** by clicking the arrow button pointing to that box. Gender is a fixed factor because it includes all levels of the factor to which the results are intended to apply – male and female are not merely a sample of levels from the gender factor (we'll explain this in a moment). Click **audience** on the left and move it to the same **Fixed Factor(s)** by clicking the arrow button pointing to that box.

◆ If you had any factors with levels that were merely a sample from the range of levels to which you wanted your results to apply, for example high, medium, and low extraversion scores, where you wanted your results to apply to people of all levels of extraversion, then you would have put them in the **Random Factor(s)** box. If you were carrying out analysis of covariance (ANCOVA), you would have put your covariate variables in the box labelled **Covariate(s)**. If you were performing a weighted least-squares analysis, you would have put the variable listing the weights in the box labelled **WLS Weight**.

◆ If you wanted a customized statistical model, you could click **Model...**, and a subdialog box would open in which you could specify the desired model. The default is a full factorial model, with all main effects and all factor-by-factor interactions included. This is the usual form of ANOVA, and you should not change it unless you know what you're doing. If you wanted to include the a priori test for differences between levels of one or both factors, you could click **Contrasts...** to open a subdialog box in which you could specify the a priori contrasts that you wanted.

◆ It is always a good idea to plot an interaction graph, in case you need to interpret a significant interaction, so click **Plots...** and the Profile Plots subdialog box will open.

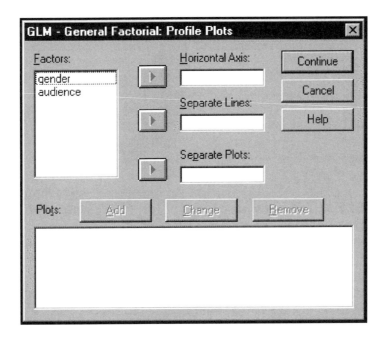

◆ The most logical plot would have the three audience conditions along the horizontal axis and separate lines on the plot for male and female students who served as subjects or experimental participants. Click the factor **audience** on the left and move it to the box labelled **Horizontal axis** by clicking the top arrow button. Click the factor **gender** on the left and move it to the box labelled **Separate lines** by clicking the arrow button pointing to that box. Click **Add**, and the two factors will appear in the box at the bottom. Click **Continue**.

◆ Back in the GLM – General Factorial (or Univariate) dialog box, click **Post Hoc...** and the General Factorial: Post Hoc Multiple Comparisons for Observed Means subdialog box will open. We made some general comments on the various types of *post hoc* or a posteriori multiple comparison tests in section 9.3, and there's no need to repeat them here. A multiple comparison test makes no sense on a factor such as gender that has only two levels, because a significant main effect for such a factor does not require further analysis, but if you have a significant main effect for audience, which has three levels, you will want to know where the differences lie, so click the factor **audience** on the left, use the arrow button to move it to the box labelled **Post Hoc Tests for**, then select **Tukey** by clicking its check box. Click **Continue**.

◆ Back in the GLM – General Factorial (or Univariate) dialog box, you could if you wished click **Save...** to save predicted values, residuals, or diagnostic

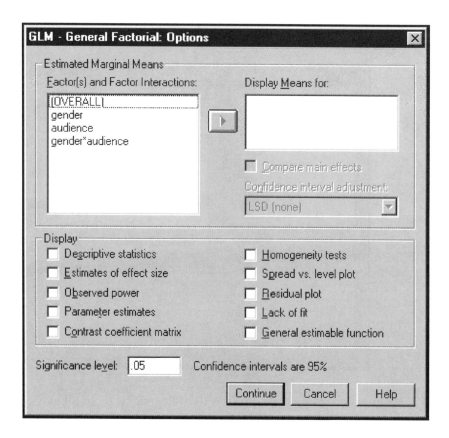

statistics, but these are not often required. Click **Options...** and the Options subdialog box will open.

◆ It is always useful to have group means, so in the Options subdialog box click the factor **gender** on the left and move it to the box labelled **Display** **M**eans **for** on the right by clicking the arrow button, then repeat the process for the factor **audience**. You could also, if you wished, ask for other descriptive statistics, estimates of effect size, observed power, homogeneity of variance tests, and various other things, and you could change the significance level from the default of .05. For now just click **Continue**.

◆ Back once again in the GLM – General Factorial (or Univariate) dialog box, click **OK**, and the results will be displayed in the SPSS Viewer. To print a hard copy of the output, follow the procedure described in section 3.2.

10.4 RESULTS

➡ Univariate Analysis of Variance

Between-Subjects Factors

		Value Label	N
GENDER	1	women	36
	2	men	36
AUDIENCE	1		24
	2		24
	3		24

Tests of Between-Subjects Effects

Dependent Variable: SCORE

Source	Type III Sum of Squares	df	Mean Square	F	Sig.
Corrected Model	8239.403[a]	5	1647.881	10.766	.000
Intercept	88102.027	1	88102.027	575.581	.000
GENDER	3758.445	1	3758.445	24.554	.000
AUDIENCE	3381.234	2	1690.617	11.045	.000
GENDER * AUDIENCE	1099.723	2	549.862	3.592	.033
Error	10102.370	66	153.066		
Total	106443.800	72			
Corrected Total	18341.773	71			

a. R Squared = .449 (Adjusted R Squared = .407)

Estimated Marginal Means

1. GENDER

Dependent Variable: SCORE

| GENDER | Mean | Std. Error | 95% Confidence Interval | |
			Lower Bound	Upper Bound
women	27.756	2.062	23.639	31.872
men	42.206	2.062	38.089	46.322

2. AUDIENCE

Dependent Variable: SCORE

| AUDIENCE | Mean | Std. Error | 95% Confidence Interval | |
			Lower Bound	Upper Bound
1	29.150	2.525	24.108	34.192
2	44.600	2.525	39.558	49.642
3	31.192	2.525	26.149	36.234

Post Hoc Tests

AUDIENCE

Multiple Comparisons

Dependent Variable: SCORE

Tukey HSD

| (I) AUDIENCE | (J) AUDIENCE | Mean Difference (I-J) | Std. Error | Sig. | 95% Confidence Interval | |
					Lower Bound	Upper Bound
1	2	-15.450*	3.571	.000	-24.013	-6.887
	3	-2.042	3.571	.836	-10.605	6.522
2	1	15.450*	3.571	.000	6.887	24.013
	3	13.408*	3.571	.001	4.845	21.972
3	1	2.042	3.571	.836	-6.522	10.605
	2	-13.408*	3.571	.001	-21.972	-4.845

Based on observed means.

*. The mean difference is significant at the .05 level.

Homogeneous Subsets

SCORE

Tukey HSD [a,b]

AUDIENCE	N	Subset 1	Subset 2
1	24	29.150	
3	24	31.192	
2	24		44.600
Sig.		.836	1.000

Means for groups in homogeneous subsets are displayed.
Based on Type III Sum of Squares
The error term is Mean Square(Error) = 153.066.

    a. Uses Harmonic Mean Sample Size = 24.000.

    b. Alpha = .05.

Profile Plots

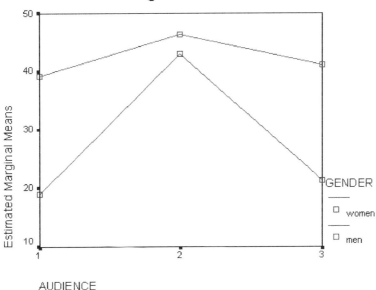

Estimated Marginal Means of SCORE

The first table of the output, labelled Between-Subjects Factors, merely summarizes the factors, showing how they were labelled and how many scores there are in each group.

The second table, labelled Tests of Between-Subjects Effects, is a standard ANOVA table with a few additions. The first column lists the sources of variation analysed.

The main body of the table lists, among other things, the sum of squares, degrees of freedom (df), mean square, value of F, and significance of F (Sig.) of each of the factors individually and also of the Gender × Audience interaction (which appears in the table as GENDER*AUDIENCE). It is clear that both of the main effects are significant at .000 (which you should interpret as less than .001) and that the Gender × Audience interaction is also significant at .033.

The following two tables, under the general heading Estimated Marginal Means, show the two means for the gender factor and the three means for the audience factor, together with their standard errors and 95 per cent confidence intervals.

The last two tables, under the general heading Post Hoc Tests, display the results of the multiple comparisons on the audience factor. We explained the meaning of these slightly mysterious tables in section 9.4. They show that mean time on target was significantly greater in the female audience condition than in the alone or the male audience condition, and that no other pairwise differences on levels of the audience factor were significant.

The last item of output is the interaction graph showing mean time on target of the women and men students in each of the three audience conditions, and it is useful having this plot, because the interaction is significant and it needs to be interpreted. We'll tell you more about drawing graphs in section 13.4.

The usual way of reporting these results is to say something like the following. The mean score of the male subjects ($M = 42.21$) was higher than the mean score of the women subjects ($M = 27.76$), and this difference was significant: $F(1, 66) = 24.55$, $p < .001$. The main effect of audience condition was also significant, $F(2, 66) = 11.05$, $p < .001$, with the highest scores in the female audience condition ($M = 44.60$) compared with the male audience ($M = 31.19$) and the alone condition ($M = 29.15$). A posteriori Tukey-HSD tests showed that the mean for the female audience condition was significantly higher than the means for the other two audience conditions ($p < .05$, two-tailed) and that no other pairwise differences on levels of this factor were significant. Finally, the Gender × Audience interaction was significant, $F(2, 66) = 3.59$, $p < .05$.

Interactions are notoriously difficult to interpret, and explaining what they mean is an art as well as a science. We find it helpful to think about interactions as follows. A main effect is a significant difference between two or more means; a two-way interaction is a significant difference between two or more *differences* between means; a three-way interaction is a significant difference between two or more differences between two or more differences between means, and so on, but from that point on the idea begins to become too complex to grasp. It is always helpful to examine the interaction graph. In the data you have just analysed, the differences between the mean scores of men and women differ quite sharply from one audience condition to the next, so there are differences between these differences, and that is why the interaction effect is significant – the interpretation is fairly obvious from the graph.

In the article from which the data were taken, the interaction was interpreted as follows: "With a female audience, female subjects' scores were similar to those of male subjects, but when working alone or in the presence of a male audience, female subjects' scores were vastly worse than those of male subjects" (Corston and Colman, 1996, pp. 166–7). Another way of interpreting the interaction would be to say that female audiences had a positive effect, especially on the performance of women subjects, but male audiences had roughly the same effect as no audience at all. In other words, the male spectator, who was in fact one of the authors of this book, functioned like a nebbish. According to a popular definition of this Yiddish word, when a nebbish enters a room, you feel as if someone has just left.

◆ If you want to go straight on to the next chapter, click **File** in the menu bar near the top of the SPSS Viewer window, then **New**, then **Data**. If you want to exit from SPSS, click **File** and then **Exit**. In either case, when you are prompted, make sure that the input data in the Data Editor are saved under the filename **genaud.sav**, because we'll need them again in section 13.4 when we tell you more about drawing graphs.

11 Repeated-Measures Analysis of Variance

11.1 BACKGROUND

One-way ANOVA with repeated measures is, in effect, an extension of the paired-samples t-test, described in chapter 7, the difference being that the means of more than two related samples are compared simultaneously. Data that require analysis using this procedure most often arise when three or more measurements of a variable are taken from a single group of individuals at different times. The situation is slightly more complicated when a multifactorial ANOVA includes one or more repeated-measures factors. The data that you're going to analyse in this chapter, for example, come from a 2×3 factorial experiment in which one factor was a between-subjects factor and the other was a within-subjects factor, that is, a repeated-measures factor. Experimental designs of this type are sometimes called mixed designs or split-plot designs.

If we show you how to analyse the data from this two-way mixed ANOVA with repeated measures on one factor, then you shouldn't find it difficult to adapt the technique for one-way repeated-measures designs, which are simpler, or for multifactorial designs with repeated measures on more than one factor, which are more complicated but involve merely duplicating, for each repeated-measures factor, the procedure that we'll describe for the single repeated-measures factor in this chapter. It should be fairly obvious once you've analysed the data below. But please note that you will not be able to perform repeated-measures ANOVA unless your version of SPSS for Windows includes the Advanced Statistics add-on enhancement.

Colman (1982, pp. 184–90) reported an experiment designed in part to investigate framing effects on cooperative decisions in social dilemmas. A social dilemma is a decision problem in which members of a group each face a choice between a cooperative choice that benefits the group as a whole and an uncooperative choice that benefits the individual at the expense of the group, and the pursuit of individual self-interest by every group member leaves everyone worse off than if they had all acted cooperatively. In one treatment condition the social dilemma was framed as an abstract decision problem, and in another it was framed as a lifelike decision problem, but the two versions were strategically equivalent, the only difference being the framing or description of the dilemma to the group members. In both framing conditions, the group members made a series of 30 decisions, which were divided into three blocks of 10 decisions each. The total numbers of cooperative choices in each of the 20 groups were as shown in Table 11.1.

The unit of analysis is the group, so think of each of the 20 groups as a separate subject, each subject being able to make between zero and 30 cooperative choices in each trial block.

11.2 DATA INPUT

For repeated-measures ANOVA, the scores are not entered into a single column of the Data Editor, as would be required for a standard randomized-groups ANOVA

Table 11.1 Social dilemmas

	Group	Trial Block 1	Trial Block 2	Trial Block 3
Abstract	1	11	8	4
	2	12	10	9
	3	20	18	13
	4	14	9	3
	5	14	6	11
	6	13	6	7
	7	10	10	7
	8	9	8	4
	9	14	16	11
	10	12	8	5
Lifelike	11	7	5	6
	12	8	5	6
	13	7	3	1
	14	3	0	0
	15	5	0	0
	16	14	9	10
	17	5	6	7
	18	7	2	1
	19	12	7	4
	20	11	8	5

such as the one we showed you in chapter 10. The data must be entered so that the repeated measures from each case (usually each individual subject, but in this data set each case is one of the 20 groups) appear in a single row, as they do in the table immediately above. The different levels of the between-subjects factor(s), however, are set out one below the other, again as in Table 11.1, and a grouping variable is used to indicate which group each row of scores belongs to. Here's what you need to do.

◆ Before keying in the scores and the grouping variable, name the variables so that the output is properly labelled and understandable. Double-click the word **var** at the top of the first column, and the familiar Define Variable dialog box will open.

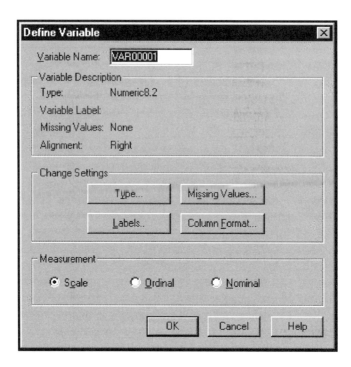

◆ In the Define Variable dialog box, the text box labelled **Variable Name** shows the default name of the first variable: VAR00001. Type the variable name **group** in the **Variable Name** text box to replace the default name VAR00001.

◆ Click **Labels...** and the Define Labels subdialog box will open.

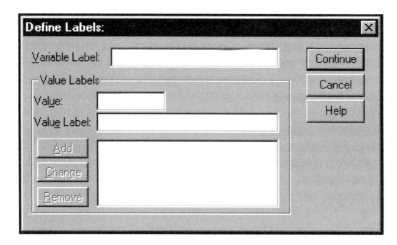

◆ Click in the text box labelled **Value** and type the numeral **1**. Click in the text box labelled **Value Label** and type **abstract**, then click **Add**. Repeat the process to define the value 2: in the text box labelled **Value** type the numeral

2, then click in the text box labelled **Valu̲e Label** and type `lifelike`, then click **A̲dd**. Click **Continue**, and you will be returned to the Define Variable dialog box.

◆ Click **OK** to get back to the Data Editor window, where you will find that the first column is now headed **group**.

◆ Double-click the word **var** at the top of the second column, and when the Define Variable dialog box opens type the variable name `block1` in the **V̲ariable Name** text box to replace the default name. This is not a grouping variable, so you don't need to define any labels. Click **OK**, and repeat the same procedure to name the third column `block2` and the fourth column `block3`.

◆ In the Define Variable dialog box there are three other buttons you could use to open subdialog boxes that are occasionally useful. **Type...** opens a subdialog box in which you could define the type of data if they were not ordinary numeric scores (which is the default); **Mi̲ssing Values...** opens a subdialog box in which you could inform SPSS about missing values, if you had any (the default setting is **N̲o missing values**); and **Column F̲ormat...** opens a subdialog box in which you could alter the display of data in the Data Editor, if for example you had scores that required a column width greater than eight characters in the Data Editor. But for most purposes the defaults are all you need, and these subdialog boxes can be ignored.

◆ When you have finished naming the variables, key in the data from the table above. The data should be set out in the Data Editor as follows:

	group	block1	block2	block3
1	1.00	11.00	8.00	4.00
2	1.00	12.00	10.00	9.00
3	1.00	20.00	18.00	13.00
4	1.00	14.00	9.00	3.00
5	1.00	14.00	6.00	11.00
6	1.00	13.00	6.00	7.00
11	2.00	7.00	5.00	6.00
12	2.00	8.00	5.00	6.00
13	2.00	7.00	3.00	1.00
14	2.00	3.00	.00	.00
15	2.00	5.00	.00	.00
16	2.00	14.00	9.00	10.00

◆ Save the data on disk for future reference by following the procedure described in section 2.6. Call the file **dilemmas.sav**.

11.3 ANALYSIS

Performing repeated-measures ANOVA is a lot easier in SPSS 8 and SPSS 9 than in previous versions of SPSS, provided you have the Advanced Statistics add-on enhancement.

◆ Click **Statistics** (or **Analyze**) in the menu bar near the top of the Data Editor, and in the drop-down menu that appears click **General Linear Model**.

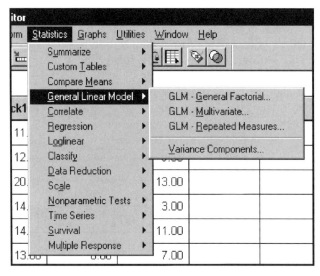

◆ Click **GLM – Repeated Measures...**, and the GLM – Repeated Measures Define Factor(s) dialog box will open. If you have only the Base System of SPSS, this command won't appear on the drop-down submenu, and you won't be able to select it.

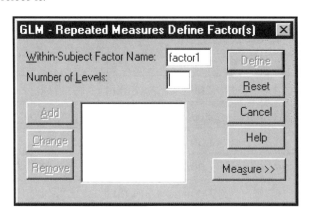

◆ You have to define a repeated-measures factor in this dialog box, and you can't simply use an existing factor name. In the text box labelled **Within-Subject Factor Name** type `trials`. Now tell SPSS how many levels this factor has. Click in the text box labelled **Number of Levels** and type **3**. Now click **Add**, and **trials(3)** will appear in the list of repeated-measures factors. Because you have only one repeated-measures factor, you can stop there. If you had more repeated-measures factors, you would have to repeat this procedure. If you were using a multivariate design with more than one dependent variable, you would need to click **Measure>>**, but for now just click **Define**, and the main GLM – Repeated Measures dialog box will appear.

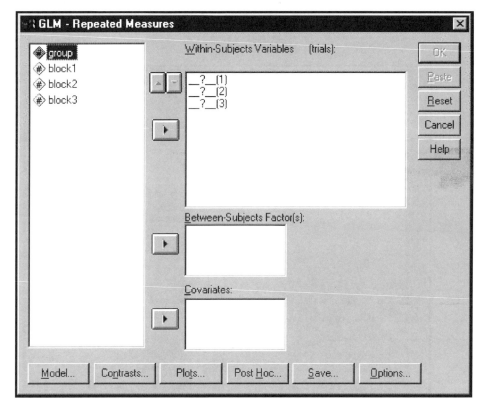

◆ In the GLM – Repeated Measures dialog box, the box labelled **Within-Subjects Variables** on the right is obviously begging for three items of information: it has _?_ repeated three times within it. Move **block1**, **block2**, and **block3** in that order from the box on the left to the **Within-Subjects Variables** box on the right by clicking to highlight each of them and then clicking the black arrow button between them. Properly speaking, these are the three levels of your within-subjects factor, so the order is crucial.

◆ Move **group** from the left to the box labelled **Between-Subjects Factor(s)** by clicking it and then clicking the appropriate arrow button. If you were carrying out a repeated-measures analysis of covariance (ANCOVA), then at this point you would have to put your covariate or covariates in the box labelled **Covariates**.

◆ If you wanted a customized statistical model, you could click **Model...**, and a subdialog box would open in which you could specify the desired model. The default is a full factorial model, with all main effects and all factor-by-factor interactions included, and this is the usual form of ANOVA. If you wanted to include the a priori test for differences between levels of one or both factors, you could click **Contrasts...** to open a subdialog box in which you could specify the a priori contrasts that you wanted. If you wanted a graph of the results, you could click **Plots...**, and if you wanted to save predicted values, residuals, or diagnostic statistics you could click **Save...**, but these are seldom required.

◆ Click **Options...** and the GLM – Repeated Measures: Options subdialog box will open.

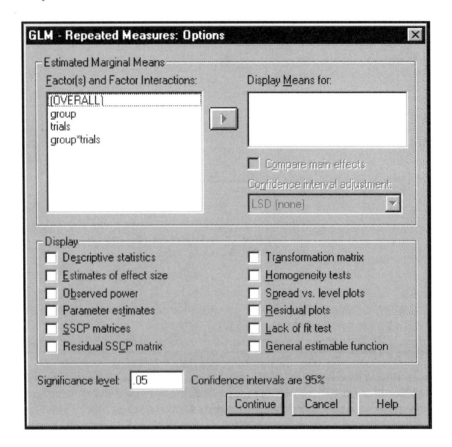

◆ It is always useful to have group means, so in the GLM – Repeated Measures: Options subdialog box click the factor **group** on the left and move it to the box labelled **Display Means for** on the right by clicking the arrow button, then repeat the process for the factor **trials**. You could also, if you wished, ask for other descriptive statistics, estimates of effect size, observed power, homogeneity of variance tests, and various other things, and you could change the significance level from the default of .05. For now just click **Continue**.

◆ Back once again in the GLM – Repeated Measures dialog box, click **OK**, and the results will be displayed in the SPSS Viewer.

◆ To print a hard copy of the output, follow the procedure described in section 3.2.

11.4 RESULTS

General Linear Model

Within-Subjects Factors

Measure: MEASURE_1

TRIALS	Dependent Variable
1	BLOCK1
2	BLOCK2
3	BLOCK3

Between-Subjects Factors

		Value Label	N
GROUP	1.00	abstract	10
	2.00	lifelike	10

Multivariate Tests[b]

Effect		Value	F	Hypothesis df	Error df	Sig.
TRIALS	Pillai's Trace	.769	28.373[a]	2.000	17.000	.000
	Wilks' Lambda	.231	28.373[a]	2.000	17.000	.000
	Hotelling's Trace	3.338	28.373[a]	2.000	17.000	.000
	Roy's Largest Root	3.338	28.373[a]	2.000	17.000	.000
TRIALS * GROUP	Pillai's Trace	.144	1.435[a]	2.000	17.000	.265
	Wilks' Lambda	.856	1.435[a]	2.000	17.000	.265
	Hotelling's Trace	.169	1.435[a]	2.000	17.000	.265
	Roy's Largest Root	.169	1.435[a]	2.000	17.000	.265

a. Exact statistic

b.
  Design: Intercept+GROUP
  Within Subjects Design: TRIALS

Mauchly's Test of Sphericity[b]

Measure: MEASURE_1

Within Subjects Effect	Mauchly's W	Approx. Chi-Square	df	Sig.	Epsilon[a]		
					Greenhouse-Geisser	Huynh-Feldt	Lower-bound
TRIALS	.989	.194	2	.907	.989	1.000	.500

Tests the null hypothesis that the error covariance matrix of the orthonormalized transformed dependent variables is proportional to an identity matrix.

a. May be used to adjust the degrees of freedom for the averaged tests of significance. Corrected tests are displayed in the layers (by default) of the Tests of Within Subjects Effects table.

b.

Design: Intercept+GROUP
Within Subjects Design: TRIALS

Tests of Within-Subjects Effects

Measure: MEASURE_1

Source		Type III Sum of Squares	df	Mean Square	F	Sig.
TRIALS	Sphericity Assumed	230.533	2	115.267	32.351	.000
	Greenhouse-Geisser	230.533	1.978	116.577	32.351	.000
	Huynh-Feldt	230.533	2.000	115.267	32.351	.000
	Lower-bound	230.533	1.000	230.533	32.351	.000
TRIALS * GROUP	Sphericity Assumed	11.200	2	5.600	1.572	.222
	Greenhouse-Geisser	11.200	1.978	5.664	1.572	.222
	Huynh-Feldt	11.200	2.000	5.600	1.572	.222
	Lower-bound	11.200	1.000	11.200	1.572	.226
Error(TRIALS)	Sphericity Assumed	128.267	36	3.563		
	Greenhouse-Geisser	128.267	35.595	3.603		
	Huynh-Feldt	128.267	36.000	3.563		
	Lower-bound	128.267	18.000	7.126		

Tests of Within-Subjects Contrasts

Measure: MEASURE_1

Source	TRIALS	Type III Sum of Squares	df	Mean Square	F	Sig.
TRIALS	Linear	220.900	1	220.900	56.240	.000
	Quadratic	9.633	1	9.633	3.012	.100
TRIALS * GROUP	Linear	6.400	1	6.400	1.629	.218
	Quadratic	4.800	1	4.800	1.501	.236
Error(TRIALS)	Linear	70.700	18	3.928		
	Quadratic	57.567	18	3.198		

Tests of Between-Subjects Effects

Measure: MEASURE_1

Transformed Variable: Average

Source	Type III Sum of Squares	df	Mean Square	F	Sig.
Intercept	3619.267	1	3619.267	127.906	.000
GROUP	317.400	1	317.400	11.217	.004
Error	509.333	18	28.296		

Estimated Marginal Means

1. GROUP

Measure: MEASURE_1

GROUP	Mean	Std. Error	95% Confidence Interval	
			Lower Bound	Upper Bound
abstract	10.067	.971	8.026	12.107
lifelike	5.467	.971	3.426	7.507

2. TRIALS

Measure: MEASURE_1

TRIALS	Mean	Std. Error	95% Confidence Interval	
			Lower Bound	Upper Bound
1	10.400	.726	8.875	11.925
2	7.200	.809	5.501	8.899
3	5.700	.768	4.086	7.314

The output from this procedure is voluminous and slightly confusing, with much information that you don't need, but you won't find it difficult to pick out the wheat from the chaff once we've talked you through this example.

The first table in the SPSS Viewer, labelled **Within-Subjects Factors** merely confirms that there is just one repeated-measures factor called TRIALS, with the three variables BLOCK1, BLOCK2, and BLOCK3 defining the three levels of the factor. The second table, labelled **Between-Subjects Factors**, confirms that there is one between-subjects factor, called GROUP, with value labels abstract and lifelike for the two levels of the factor, and $N = 10$ in each group.

The third table, **Multivariate Tests**, can be ignored, because the data in this analysis are univariate rather than multivariate – there is just one dependent variable, namely the number of cooperative choices per group per trial block.

The fourth table, **Mauchly's Test of Sphericity**, should not be ignored. It displays the results of a test of certain important homogeneity-of-variance assumptions about the variance-covariance matrix of the dependent variable. If the significance of Mauchly's W is small (usually taken to mean less than .05), then the assumptions are not met and an adjustment needs to be made to the degrees of freedom to draw conclusions from the ANOVA – both the numerator and the denominator degrees of freedom must be multiplied by one of the three values of epsilon shown in the table (the Greenhouse–Geisser epsilon is the most popular), and the mean square, F ratio, and significance of F must be evaluated with these new degrees of freedom. In this case, the significance of Mauchly's W is high (.907), so the assumptions are met and no adjustments are needed.

The fifth table, **Tests of Within-Subjects Effects**, shows the sum of squares, degrees of freedom (df), mean square, F, and significance level of F (Sig.) of the repeated-measures factor (trials) and the Trials × Group interaction. In both cases, the values are given first with sphericity assumed (see the previous paragraph), and then with each of three possible adjustments to the degrees of freedom using different values of epsilon in case the sphericity assumption was not met. In this case, the sphericity assumption was met, so we may use the values with sphericity assumed and ignore the rest. For the repeated-measures factor trials, F is given as 32.351 and the significance of F as .000 (less than .001), and for the Trials × Group interaction, F is given as 1.572 and the significance of F as .222.

The sixth table, **Tests of Within-Subjects Contrasts**, provides estimates of the linear and curvilinear trend across levels of the repeated-measures factor (trials) and the Trials × Group interaction differences. In this case the linear trend in the trials factor is significant ($F = 56.24$, $p < .001$), suggesting that the number of cooperative choices changed steadily or evenly over trial blocks, and the quadratic trend is not significant ($F = 3.01$, $p > .05$). There are no significant trends in the Trials × Group interaction differences.

The seventh table, **Tests of Between-Subjects Effects**, displays the sum of squares, degrees of freedom (df), F, and significance level of F (Sig.) of the between-subjects factor (group). For this factor, the F ratio is given as 11.217 and the significance level as .004.

The last two tables, grouped under the heading **Estimated Marginal Means**, show the means for the Abstract and Lifelike treatment groups and for the three trial blocks of the repeated-measures factor, together with standard errors and 95 per cent confidence intervals.

In a journal article or research monograph, we would report the results of the analysis as follows. A significant main effect due to the framing of the social dilemma was observed. The mean number of cooperative choices per trial block was higher in the Abstract framing group ($M = 10.07$) than in the Lifelike framing group ($M = 5.47$), and this difference was significant: $F(1, 18) = 11.22$, $p = .004$. There was a decline in the mean number of cooperative choices across trial blocks, with $M = 10.40$ in Trial Block 1, $M = 7.20$ in Trial Block 2, and $M = 5.70$ in Trial Block 3, and the differences between these three means were significant: $F(2, 36) = 32.35$, $p < .001$. The Trial Block × Group interaction was not significant: $F(2, 36) = 1.57$, $p > .05$.

It would be nice to report the results of *post hoc* multiple comparisons between the three trial block means, but unfortunately there is no way to request such tests automatically in SPSS following a repeated-measures ANOVA, and the most popular multiple comparison tests, such as the Tukey-HSD test, are in any case not designed for repeated-measures data. The way forward is to perform a separate paired-samples *t*-test on each pair of means of the trial blocks factor, using the method described in section 7.3 and ignoring the group factor by pooling the scores from both groups, but applying the Bonferroni correction to the significance level to protect against a Type I error arising from the use of repeated tests. With the present data you would have to perform three *t*-tests, because you'd have to compare the means of Trial Block 1 with Trial Block 2, Trial Block 1 with Trial Block 3, and Trial Block 2 with Trial Block 3. To achieve a conventional significance level of $p < .05$ for the three tests taken together, you would have to apply a Bonferroni-corrected significance level of .05/3 (that is, .017) to each separate *t*-test. You would then report the multiple comparisons as Bonferroni *t*-test results using a familywise significance level of $p < .05$. If you were comparing four means, then you'd have six pairwise *t*-tests to perform, and to maintain a familywise significance level of $p < .05$ you'd use a significance level of .05/6 (.008) for each separate Bonferroni *t*-test.

◆ If you want to go straight on to the next chapter, click **File** in the menu bar near the top of the SPSS Viewer, then **New**, then **Data**. If you want to exit from SPSS, then click **File** and then **Exit**. When prompted, save the input data for future reference under the filename **dilemmas.sav** if you have not done so already.

12 Multiple Regression

12.1 BACKGROUND

Multiple regression (or multiple linear regression analysis, to give it its full name) is an extension or generalization of the basic bivariate (two-variable) technique of linear regression analysis that was originally put forward in a primitive form by Francis Galton, half-cousin of the biologist Charles Darwin, at a meeting of the Royal Institution in London in 1877. Multiple regression is a statistical technique for analysing the separate and joint influences of two or more independent variables, also called predictor variables, on a dependent variable. The general form of a multiple regression equation for k independent variables is a weighted sum:

$$\hat{Y} = \beta_0 + \beta_1 X_1 + \beta_2 X_2 + \ldots + \beta_k X_k.$$

In this equation, $\hat{Y}$ (hat or Y circumflex) is the *predicted* (hence the hat) score on the dependent variable, each X_i is one of the independent variables, β_0 is the intercept – the value of $\hat{Y}$ when all of the $X_i = 0$ – and each β_i ($i = 1$ to k) is a standardized regression coefficient indicating the relative importance of the corresponding independent variable in determining the predicted value of the dependent variable. The standardized regression coefficients are often called beta weights, because the letter β in the equation is the lower-case letter beta, the second letter of the Greek alphabet. Sometimes the symbol B is used instead of β, especially for unstandardized regression coefficients, and although it looks identical to the second letter of the Roman alphabet, it is in fact an upper-case Greek beta. Regression analysis calculates the intercept and regression coefficients so as to provide the best-fitting linear equation according to the least-squares criterion, that is, such that the sum of the squared deviations of the predicted scores from the observed scores is minimized to give the most accurate prediction. The multiple regression procedure is one of the largest and most complex in SPSS, but that isn't a cause for alarm, although it does make it difficult for us to summarize briefly. We'll deal with it as straightforwardly as we can without omitting too many important details.

The data shown in Table 12.1 are taken from the Research Assessment Exercise carried out by the Universities Funding Council (UFC) in the United Kingdom in 1993 (Universities Funding Council, 1993). We have chosen the ratings of anthropology departments, because there were only 17 of them in the assessment exercise and it shouldn't take you too long to key in the data. But it will take a few minutes, so do be patient – you need a reasonable amount of data to perform a meaningful multiple regression analysis.

Let us first explain the data. The first column simply labels each of the universities with anthropology departments – we've omitted their names to save their blushes. The second column is the dependent variable, namely the ratings of research performance awarded by the UFC to the anthropology departments on a scale from 1 (worst) to 5 (best). The following five columns contain the performance indicators that were used in the Research Assessment Exercise and that you are about to subject to multiple regression analysis:

Table 12.1 Research assessment exercise

Univ	Rating	Staffing	Pubs	Articles	ABRC	Grants
1	4	6.75	13.56	2.52	13464	2856
2	5	28.25	21.29	4.46	21401	9561
3	4	10.50	13.08	3.36	95	582
4	4	13.00	9.15	1.42	16050	5814
5	3	7.50	10.17	1.73	716	8161
6	5	19.75	10.22	1.77	13070	10706
7	5	19.50	15.17	1.67	2053	3562
8	5	20.75	16.17	2.55	6680	5608
9	5	12.25	16.67	1.80	3384	2994
10	5	29.00	13.96	2.58	13261	26351
11	2	4.50	25.38	3.22	3678	15853
12	4	10.50	9.75	.76	472	26149
13	4	14.50	11.35	1.72	6772	7814
14	4	13.25	11.47	1.47	6699	346
15	3	6.00	5.50	2.33	6573	1144
16	1	4.50	2.89	.22	0	0
17	3	17.25	7.48	.87	0	31755

Staffing: The average number of staff members in the department over the assessment period (1988 to 1992)

Pubs: The average number of publications of all types per staff member over the assessment period (not time spent by staff members in public houses, a performance indicator that the UFC overlooked completely)

Articles: The average number of articles in academic journals per staff member over the assessment period

ABRC: Advisory Board for Research Councils, that is, research income from government research councils per staff member over the assessment period

Grants: Other external research income per staff member over the assessment period

How well could we predict a department's rating on the basis of its scores on the five independent variables? What was the relative importance of the various performance indicators in determining the ratings? To answer questions such as these you need to perform a multiple regression analysis as follows.

12.2 DATA INPUT

The data input is quite straightforward, and it is similar to data input for other procedures in SPSS, so it will not cause you problems.

◆ Begin by naming the first six columns of the Data Editor **rating**, **staffing**, **pubs**, **articles**, **abrc**, and **grants** in that order. Double-click **var** at the top of the first column, and the Define Variable dialog box, which you've met often before, will open. The text box labelled **Variable Name** will show the default name of the first variable: VAR00001. To rename it, type `rating` in the text box. Click **OK**, and you will be returned to the Data Editor, with the first column relabelled. Repeat the procedure to name the second column **staffing**, and continue in the same way until all six columns have been labelled as in Table 12.1.

◆ Key the data into their appropriate columns using the procedure described in section 2.4.

◆ Save the data on disk for future reference by following the procedure described in section 2.6. Call this data file **regress.sav**.

12.3 ANALYSIS

Performing a multiple regression analysis is quite a long and complex process, but it isn't particularly difficult once you know what you're doing.

◆ Click **Statistics** (or **Analyze**) in the menu bar near the top of the Data Editor, then click **Regression**.

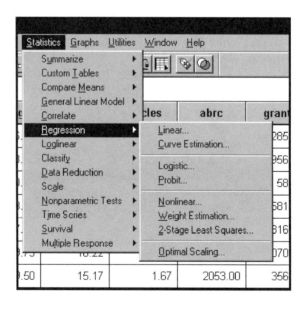

◆ Click **Linear...** and the Linear Regression dialog box will open.

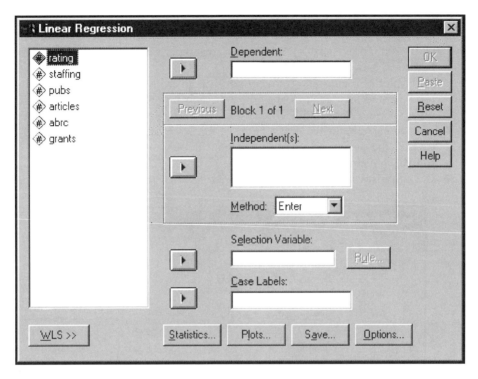

◆ Move the variable name **rating** to the **Dependent** box, because it is the dependent variable, and all the other variable names to the **Independent(s)** box, because they are independent variables. To move a variable from the list box on the left to one of the boxes on the right, click it if it isn't already highlighted, and then click the arrow button pointing to the desired destination box.

◆ If you wanted to use a method other than standard (forced entry) multiple regression, which is the default and is called **Enter**, you could click the arrow to the right of the box labelled **Method** and click one of the alternatives in the drop-down menu that would open. The alternatives are **Stepwise**, which adds and removes variables from the model according to criteria entered in the Options dialog box; **Remove**, which begins with all variables in the model and then removes variables *en bloc*; **Backward**, which removes individual variables from the model according to criteria entered in the Options dialog box until a model is reached from which no more are eligible for removal, and **Forward**, which adds individual variables to the model according to criteria entered in the Options dialog box until a model is reached from which no more are eligible for entry. The least controversial of these techniques, and the most suitable for most purposes, is the standard multiple regression technique **Enter** in which all variables are entered in a single step, and we recommend that you use it unless you have strong theoretical grounds for choosing one of the stepwise procedures (**Stepwise**, **Backward**, or **Forward**). You could choose a stepwise method simply by clicking it, but leave the default method **Enter** selected for this analysis.

◆ If you wanted to limit your analysis to a subset of cases, you could have included a grouping variable identifying these cases in the Data Editor, and you would now have to move that grouping variable to the box labelled **Se̲lection Variable**. The **C̲ase Labels** box is for identifying certain points on a scatterplot of the results. If one of your variables had been a weighting variable for weighted least-squares analysis, attaching more weight to some cases than others because they had been measured more accurately and you wanted them to have more influence in the analysis, for example, you could click **W̲LS** and transfer the weighting variable that you had entered into the Data Editor to the **WLS Weig̲ht** box.

◆ Click **S̲tatistics...** and the Linear Regression: Statistics subdialog box will open.

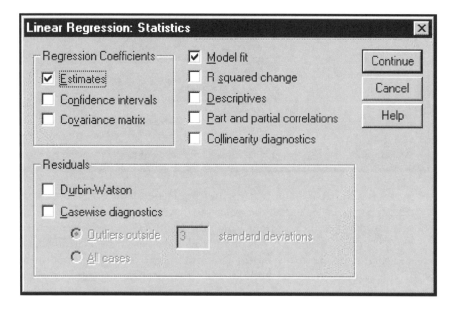

◆ In this Linear Regression: Statistics subdialog box you could click check boxes to select various additional statistics that you wished to be displayed with the output. The two items that are selected by default and are required for virtually all multiple regressions are **Estimates**, which are the regression coefficients themselves, and **Model fit** statistics, which include R^2, the coefficient of determination, which is the proportion of variance in the dependent variable that is explained by the regression equation or model. Among the additional options are **Confidence intervals**, the 95 per cent confidence intervals for the regression coefficients; **Covariance matrix**, a table showing the variance of each regression coefficient and the covariances between every pair of coefficients; **Descriptives**, the mean and standard deviation of each variable and a correlation matrix for the complete set of variables; and **Collinearity diagnostics**, including the tolerance of each variable and other statistics for diagnosing collinearity problems. The collinearity diagnostics are designed to check an assumption of multiple regression, that one independent variable is not a linear function of the others.

At the bottom of the subdialog box you will find **Durbin–Watson**, the Durbin–Watson test for serial correlation of residuals, which checks another crucial assumption of multiple regression involving observations recorded sequentially or serially, namely that the residuals of consecutive observations are uncorrelated. A residual is the observed value of the dependent variable minus the value predicted by the model. If the residuals are uncorrelated, then the Durbin–Watson statistic is 2; values close to zero or 4 indicate positive or negative correlation, respectively. Finally, there is a check box for **Casewise diagnostics** for identifying extreme scores or outliers. When you have selected the statistics you require and deselected the others (for now just select the defaults **Estimates** and **Model fit**, which are more than enough for our purposes), click **Continue**.

◆ Back in the Linear Regression dialog box, if you want the output to include scatterplots of various kinds, click **Plots...** and the Linear Regression: Plots subdialog box will open.

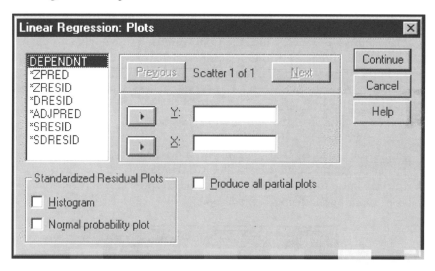

◆ In this Linear Regression: Plots subdialog box you can request a scatterplot showing the relationship between any pair of variables shown in the list box on the left. To request a scatterplot, select a variable on the left by clicking it, move it to the box labelled **Y** by clicking the appropriate arrow button if you want it to appear on the vertical axis or *Y*-axis of the scatterplot, then select another variable and move it in the same way to the box labelled **X** so that it appears on the horizontal axis or *X*-axis. One of the most useful plots is ***ZRESID**, the regression standardized residual, as a function of ***ZPRED**, the regression standardized predicted value. As we mentioned earlier, residuals are observed values of the dependent variable minus the value predicted by the model, and any standardized variable is the original variable divided by its standard error so that it is expressed in units of standard deviations. A plot of these two variables serves as a check of a key assumption of multiple regression that variances of residuals are equal across the range of the predicted values of the dependent variable. Select ***ZRESID** and move it to the box labelled **Y**, and then select ***ZPRED** and move it to the box labelled **X**. To set up another scatterplot, you could click **Next** and repeat the procedure for another pair of variables. In this dialog box you could also click check boxes to select **Histogram** to produce a histogram of the standardized residuals with a normal curve superimposed on it (to check the assumption that the residuals are normally distributed), **Normal probability plot** to display a normal probability plot of the residuals, which should be a straight line if the variable is normally distributed as is also assumed by the multiple regression procedure, and **Produce all partial plots** to display scatterplots of the residuals of each independent variable on one axis against residuals of the dependent variable on the other. Unless you're a glutton for scatterplots, we suggest you ignore these additional plots and click **Continue**.

♦ Back in the Linear Regression dialog box, if you wanted to save various new variables that SPSS calculates and places in additional columns of the Data Editor, you could click **Save...**, and you could then specify what you wanted to save in the subdialog box that would open. Especially useful are **Mahalanobis**, Mahalanobis' distance, a measure of how much a case's value on the independent variable differs from the mean of all the scores; **Cook's** distance, which is an index of how much the residuals of all scores would alter if that case were excluded from the analysis; and **Leverage values**, which are estimates of how much each individual score affects the fit of the regression model. Various influence statistics listed in the subdialog box may also be worth saving, although we have observed that in practice analysts seldom save any of these additional variables. If you are in the subdialog box, then to get back to the Linear Regression dialog box, click **Continue**.

♦ In the Linear Regression dialog box, click **Options...** and the Linear Regression: Options subdialog box will open.

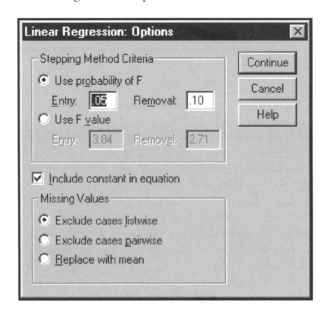

◆ In the Linear Regression: Options subdialog box, if you were using one of the stepwise regression methods (Stepwise, Backward, or Forward), you could set the criteria for entry and removal of variables. The defaults, which are generally chosen, are .05 probability for entry and .10 probability for removal. In this subdialog box you could also determine the treatment of missing values, if you had any. The default, which again is widely accepted, is listwise exclusion, which means that only those cases with valid scores on all variables are used in the analysis. Finally, you could instruct SPSS to suppress the constant term in the regression equation, producing a line through the origin, but this is seldom a good idea. We recommend that you leave the default options as they are, both in this case and generally. Click **Continue**.

◆ In the Linear Regression dialog box for the last time, click **OK**, and the SPSS Viewer window will display the results of the analysis. If some of the results scroll out of sight, use the scroll bars as explained in section 2.5. To print a hard copy of the output, follow the procedure described in section 3.2.

12.4 RESULTS

Regression

Variables Entered/Removed[b]

Model	Variables Entered	Variables Removed	Method
1	GRANTS, ABRC, PUBS, STAFFING, ARTICLES[a]	.	Enter

a. All requested variables entered.

b. Dependent Variable: RATING

Model Summary[b]

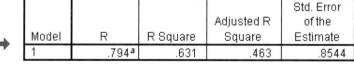

Model	R	R Square	Adjusted R Square	Std. Error of the Estimate
1	.794[a]	.631	.463	.8544

a. Predictors: (Constant), GRANTS, ABRC, PUBS, STAFFING, ARTICLES

b. Dependent Variable: RATING

ANOVA[b]

Model		Sum of Squares	df	Mean Square	F	Sig.
1	Regression	13.734	5	2.747	3.762	.031[a]
	Residual	8.031	11	.730		
	Total	21.765	16			

a. Predictors: (Constant), GRANTS, ABRC, PUBS, STAFFING, ARTICLES

b. Dependent Variable: RATING

Coefficients[a]

Model		Unstandardized Coefficients		Standardized Coefficients	t	Sig.
		B	Std. Error	Beta		
1	(Constant)	2.140	.604		3.540	.005
	STAFFING	.121	.038	.788	3.211	.008
	PUBS	4.871E-02	.060	.229	.808	.436
	ARTICLES	-.160	.355	-.143	-.451	.661
	ABRC	9.800E-06	.000	.055	.223	.828
	GRANTS	-3.29E-05	.000	-.280	-1.323	.213

a. Dependent Variable: RATING

Residuals Statistics[a]

	Minimum	Maximum	Mean	Std. Deviation	N
Predicted Value	2.7899	5.7887	3.8824	.9265	17
Residual	-1.7919	1.0882	3.918E-16	.7085	17
Std. Predicted Value	-1.179	2.058	.000	1.000	17
Std. Residual	-2.097	1.274	.000	.829	17

a. Dependent Variable: RATING

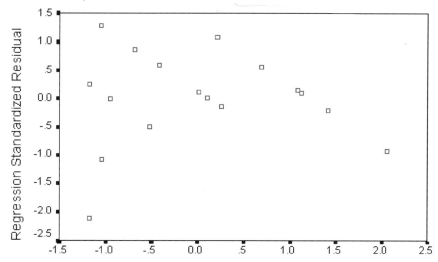

Scatterplot

Dependent Variable: RATING

The first table of the output, headed **Variables Entered/Removed**, confirms that all five of the independent variables were entered and none were removed, because you used the standard multiple regression technique and not a stepwise procedure or other nonstandard procedure.

The second table, **Model Summary**, gives the value of R, also called the coefficient of multiple correlation, R^2, also called the coefficient of determination, the adjusted R square, and the standard error of the estimate. The most important data here are the coefficient of determination, which is shown as $R^2 = .631$, and the adjusted $R^2 = .463$. The coefficient of determination R^2 is the proportion of variance in the dependent variable that is explained by the model, and it is over 63 per cent in this case. The reason for the adjusted value, which is always lower than the original R^2, is that the original is generally an overestimate, because the regression equation has been specifically tailored to fit what is usually a sample of data, and if it is applied to a new sample, it probably wouldn't fit quite as well. The adjusted $R^2 = .463$ is designed to correct for this optimistic bias. But the data used in our analysis are not sample data used to estimate population values; the anthropology departments studied were the whole population of UK anthropology departments. The unadjusted $R^2 = .631$ is therefore the right one to use, and it suggests that about 63 per cent of the variance in ratings of anthropology departments in the 1992 research assessment exercise is explained by the five independent variables that we examined.

The third table, **ANOVA**, summarizes the results of an analysis of variance, showing that the ratio of the variance (mean square) explained by the regression (2.747) to the residual or unexplained variance (.730), which is an F ratio, is $F = 3.762$, and the significance of this F ratio is $p < .031$, which is less than $p = .05$ and is therefore statistically significant by conventional standards. It is reasonable to conclude from this that the results of the analysis are not due merely to chance.

The fourth table, **Coefficients**, provides data from which you can build the regression equation or model. The unstandardized B coefficients for each of the independent variables are given first, with their standard errors, and then the standardized coefficients or beta weights are given with their t values and significance levels. Taking the variables in descending order of their standardized regression coefficients, which is good practice in reporting the results of multiple regression, the equation is as follows:

$$RATING = 2.14 + .79STAFFING - .28GRANTS + .23PUBS - .14ARTICLES + .05ABRC$$

Grants from sources other than research councils (GRANTS) and articles in academic journals (ARTICLES) appear at first to have had a *negative* effect on the departmental research ratings, but notice that these independent variables did not achieve a significance level of $p < .05$ according to the t-test results in the right-hand columns, and so their coefficients may be attributed to chance. In fact, the only independent variable that did achieve significance is STAFFING. This means that the ratings of anthropology departments were overwhelmingly influenced by the sheer sizes of the departments. This is a well-known bias that was identified in several other subject areas of the 1992 research assessment exercise.

The fifth table, **Residual Statistics**, provides some basic information about the values of the dependent variable that were predicted by the model and about the residuals or error terms.

Finally, the scatterplot that you requested of ***ZRESID**, the regression standardized residual as a function of ***ZPRED**, the regression standardized predicted value shows no evidence that the assumption of homogeneity of variance was violated. The regression standardized residuals do not increase, or decrease, or change markedly or systematically as the regression standardized predicted values increase. If they did, the results would be hard to interpret, and you would have to consider transforming the variables and then running the analysis again, but we won't venture into those deep and murky waters in this book.

◆ If you want to go straight on to the last chapter, click **File** in the menu bar near the top of the SPSS Viewer window, then **New**, then **Data**. If you want to exit from SPSS, click **File** and then **Exit**. In either case, when you are prompted, you might want to save the input data in the Data Editor under the filename **regress.sav** for future reference.

13 Charts and Graphs

13.1 BACKGROUND

The chart function within SPSS for Windows is a powerful and flexible tool that allows you to produce a wide range of graphic data summaries. Charts and graphs are produced from whatever is in the Data Editor or SPSS Viewer at the time, so there's no need to enter the data again in order to draw a chart or graph, in fact the procedure is surprisingly quick and easy, and with a little editing it is possible to produce figures that are good enough to publish in books and journals. The full range of graphic facilities available in SPSS is vast, and certainly beyond the scope of a crash course, so we'll concentrate on just a few of the main features of bar charts, pie charts, simple and multiple line graphs, and scatterplots. By the time you've finished this chapter you'll know only a little about charts and graphs but more than the majority of SPSS users.

13.2 BAR CHARTS

The estimated numbers of worshippers belonging to the major religions of the world are as shown in Table 13.1 (Henderson and Allan, 1994, p. 103).

To produce a bar chart summarizing these figures, get SPSS for Windows up and running. You will have to name the first two columns of the Data Editor **religion** and **millions**, following the procedure that you should know already but that we'll reiterate below. Then before you can key in the data you must let SPSS know that one of its columns is going to have text rather than numbers entered into it. This is how you do it.

◆ Double-click **var** at the top of the first column, and in the Define Variable dialog box that opens type **religion** in the text box labelled **Variable Name** to replace the default name VAR00001.

◆ In the same dialog box, click **Type...** and in the Define Variable Type: religion subdialog box that opens click the radio button beside **String** to select

Table 13.1   World religions

Religion	Worshippers (millions)
Christianity	1784
Islam	951
Hinduism	655
Buddhism	310
Confucianism	250
Taoism	20
Judaism	18
Sikhism	17

it. Click **Continue**, then back in the Define Variable dialog box click **OK**. This procedure enables you to type the *actual names* of the religions into columns of the Data Editor where SPSS usually expects to have *numbers* entered. A string variable, also called an alphanumeric variable, can contain letters as well as numbers, and upper and lower case letters are treated as distinct.

◆ Double-click **var** at the top of the second column, and in the Define Variable dialog box that opens type **millions** in the text box labelled **Variable Name** to replace the default name. Click **OK**.

◆ Now enter the data from Table 13.1 (review section 2.4 if you've forgotten how to do this). The first column should contain the names of the religions, shortened to a maximum of eight characters – use **Christan** and **Confuc** for the two long names. The second column should contain the numbers of worshippers belonging to each of the eight major religions. When the data have been entered into the Data Editor, save them for future reference under the file name **religion.sav** using the procedure described in section 2.6, then prepare yourself for one of the more pleasant features of SPSS. First, here's how to produce a bar chart.

◆ Click **Graphs** in the menu bar near the top of the Data Editor, and a drop-down menu will appear.

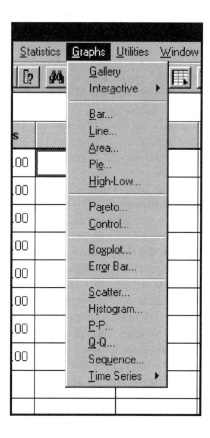

◆ Click **Bar...**, and the Bar Charts dialog box will appear.

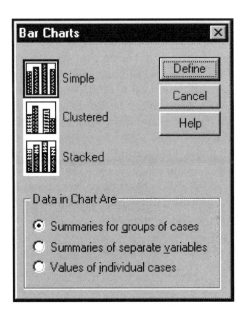

◆ Three types of bar charts are shown diagrammatically as picture buttons on the left. Select **Simple** by clicking it, and a border will appear round it. The alternatives, labelled **Clustered** and **Stacked**, are used for bar charts having more than one bar for each category, either side by side (clustered) or on top of one another (stacked), representing further subdivisions of the categories. For example, if the number of worshippers in each religion was broken down into male and female, you would need a clustered or stacked bar chart with two bars for each religion.

◆ At the bottom of the Bar Charts dialog box, select **Values of individual cases** by clicking the radio button beside it, because the data that you want to display consists of values or numbers associated with rows of the Data Editor, and each row is an individual case in the terminology of SPSS. The other types listed at the bottom of the dialog box are suitable for data sets from which SPSS must either count cases or calculate means. You would select **Summaries for groups of cases** if you had cases (rows in the Data Editor) that fell into several subgroups. For example, if there were 100 cases (rows) representing 100 individuals, and a different column of the Data Editor had the name or code of the individual's religion, then you would select **Summaries for groups of cases**, and SPSS would count the cases associated with each religious group and produce a bar chart showing the comparative counts. You would select the third alternative, **Summaries of separate variables**, if you had a different variable or set of scores in each column of the Data Editor; SPSS would calculate the mean of each variable and display the means as separate bars on a bar chart. Try to remember these alternatives; they often cause people to get stuck.

◆ Click **Define**, and a subdialog box entitled Define Simple Bar: Values of Individual Cases will open.

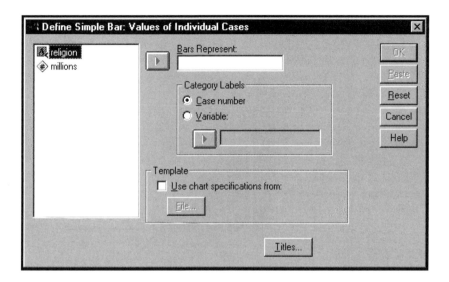

◆ The height of the bars should represent millions of worshippers, so click **millions** on the left and move it to the box labelled **Bars Represent** by clicking the upper arrow button pointing that way. Your individual cases are identified by names entered in a separate variable (column) of the Data Editor, not merely by their row or case numbers, so in the group labelled Category Labels select **Variable** by clicking its radio button. If the cases were not identified by a variable in the Data Editor containing names, you would have selected **Case number** instead. Then click **religion** on the left to highlight it, and transfer it to the box that is now labelled **Category Labels: Variable** by clicking the lower arrow button pointing towards this box.

◆ A button labelled **Titles...** at the bottom of the dialog box opens a subdialog box in which you could, if you wished, add a title and subtitle, and also a footnote, to your bar chart.

◆ In the Define Simple Bar: Values of Individual Cases dialog box, click **OK**, and after a pause the SPSS Viewer will appear with your bar chart displayed (upper graph overleaf).

◆ If you want to discard the chart, click **File** in the menu bar near the top of the SPSS Viewer and **Close** in the drop-down menu. When prompted to decide whether you want to save the contents of the SPSS Viewer, you would then click **No**. We'll tell you later how to save a chart or graph. But first, we'll show you how to edit it with the help of the SPSS Chart Editor.

◆ Double-click the chart that you want to alter, and the SPSS Chart Editor will appear (lower graph overleaf).

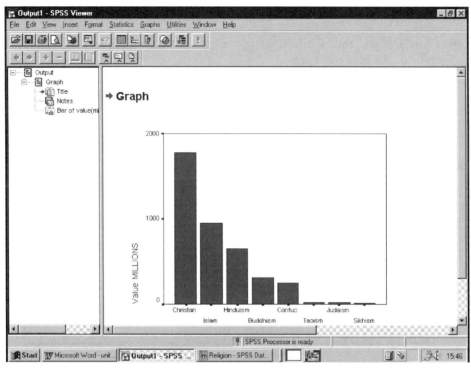

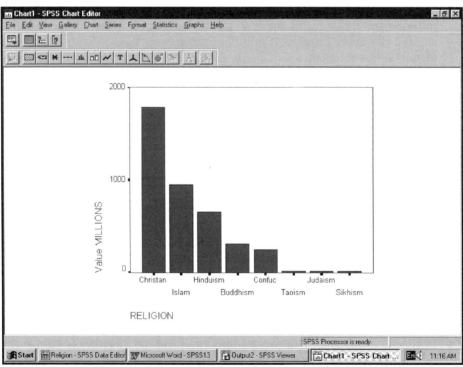

◆ In the SPSS Chart Editor, you can click some of the icons in the icon bar just below the menu bar – those that aren't available for bar charts are dimmed – and in each case a menu or dialog box will appear. If you can't understand what to do at that stage, there is generally a **Help** button available for task-specific information. In many cases you select an aspect, and then click a button marked **Apply**, but you sometimes have to click a feature of the chart or graph first so that the Chart Editor knows where to apply the selected feature. Starting from the top left of the icon bar, the icons allow the following functions to be performed:

Dialog recall:	Allows you to review recently used SPSS commands
Goto data:	Allows you to switch between the Chart Editor and the Data Editor
Go to case number:	Allows you to go immediately to a specific row of the Data Editor
Variables:	Opens a window that displays data about the variables currently in use
Point Id:	Used in conjunction with scatterplots and boxplots, activates the point selection mode and either displays or suppresses the label(s) of the case(s) selected by clicking
Fill pattern:	Allows you to alter the pattern of shaded areas: plain, striped, cross-hatched, and so on
Colour:	Allows you to alter the colour of either a border or a fill pattern
Marker:	Allows you to alter the dots, squares, triangles, open circles, or other markers that join lines in line graphs
Line styles:	Allows you to alter the thickness of lines and whether they are continuous, dotted, or broken
Bar styles:	Allows you to select plain, drop-shadow, or 3-D effect in bar graphs
Bar label styles:	Allows you to display exact numerical values to be printed above or near the top of bars in bar charts
Interpolation:	Allows you to alter methods of connecting points in certain kinds of charts and graphs
Text styles:	Allows you to choose fonts and point sizes for the text that appears with the chart or graph
3-D rotation:	Allows you to rotate the chart around one of its axes (only if it's a three-dimensional scatter plot)
Swap axes:	Allows you, in a two-dimensional chart or graph, to swap the horizontal and vertical axes
Explode slice:	Allows you to separate slices of a pie chart from the main part of the chart
Break lines at:	Allows you to break lines where there are missing values in your data
Chart options:	Allows access to further options for some kinds of charts and graphs

Set/exit spin mode: Allows charts and graphs to be turned or spun about an axis

◆ A short-cut method available for some editing functions is to double-click the feature of the chart or graph that you want to alter, and a relevant dialog box will open immediately. We'll show you a couple of examples that are often useful.

◆ Double-click the label on the vertical axis, which appears as **Value MIL-LIONS**, and the Scale Axis dialog box will open automatically.

◆ By replacing what appears in the text box labelled **Axis Title**, you can alter the label of the vertical axis to **MILLIONS**. Just click inside the text box and delete the unwanted characters or retype the desired label. Now alter the alignment of the label so that it is centred on the vertical axis, which will look better. The box labelled **Title Justification** shows the default justification as **Left/bottom**. Click the little arrow on the right of this box, and a list of alternatives will drop down. Click **Center** in this list. Then click **OK**, and the amended label will be centred. Next, centre the label **RELIGION** on the horizontal axis by double-clicking it and using the Scale Axis dialog box. To leave the Chart Editor at this point, click **File** in the menu bar near the top of the window, then **Close**, and you will be returned to the SPSS Viewer. If you find yourself in the Data Editor, click **Window** in the menu bar and then select the SPSS Viewer by clicking it in the drop-down menu.

◆ To print the chart, click **File** in the menu bar near the top of the SPSS Chart Editor, and then click **Print...**, and the Print dialog box will open.

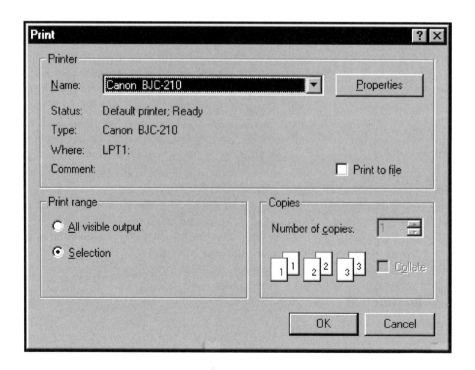

◆ In the Print dialog box you have two main options: you can print everything in the current display in the SPSS Viewer by clicking the radio button **All visible output,** or you can print only the items currently selected by clicking the radio button **Selection**. It is usually best to select what you want printed by clicking the mouse. Your bar chart is probably still selected, with handles and a box round it. If not click inside it once. Click **OK** and the chart will be printed out.

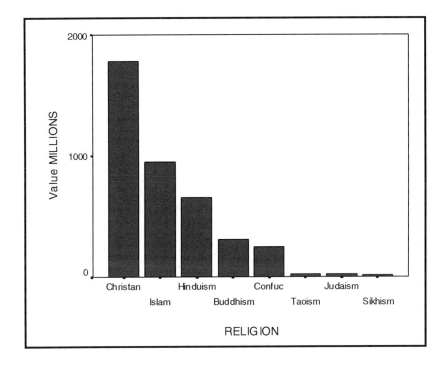

The bar chart shows the relative numbers of worshippers very vividly, in a way that makes a much stronger impression than the mere numbers themselves – to paraphrase a Chinese proverb, one picture is worth at least eight numbers. This particular bar chart conveys an ego-inflating message for Christians and a humbling one for Taoists, Jews, and Sikhs.

◆ You may save the chart by clicking **File** in the menu bar near the top of the SPSS Viewer and then **Save As...**, and the Save As dialog box will open.

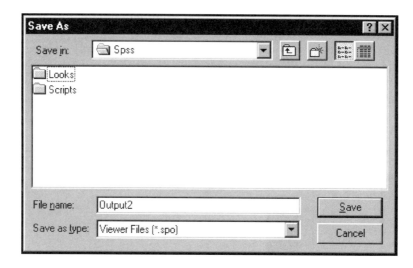

♦ Select the drive with the disk on which you want to save the chart by clicking the little arrow on the right of the box labelled **Save in** and then clicking the drive name, probably **3½ Floppy (A:)**, in the drop-down menu. An SPSS chart or graph must always be saved with the file name extension **.spo**. Type a file name such as **religion.spo** in the text box marked **File name**, then click **Save** and wait for the file to be saved. We ought to warn you that charts and graphs take up a lot of disk space, and if you try to save many of them on a floppy disk you may run out of storage space. Don't exit from SPSS yet, because we're going to show you how to display the same information in different ways.

13.3 PIE CHARTS AND SIMPLE LINE GRAPHS

Now you're going to display the same data set as a pie chart. Later on you'll transform it into a simple line graph.

♦ Click **Graphs** in the menu bar near the top of the SPSS Viewer. In the menu that drops down select **Pie...**, and the Pie Charts dialog box will open.

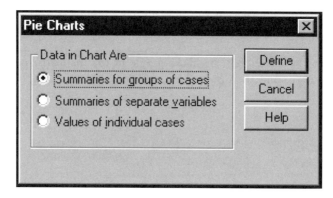

◆ In the Pie Charts dialog box, click the radio button labelled **Values of individual cases** (we explained the reasons for this in section 13.2). Click the button marked **Define**, and a subdialog box called Define Pie: Values of Individual Cases will open.

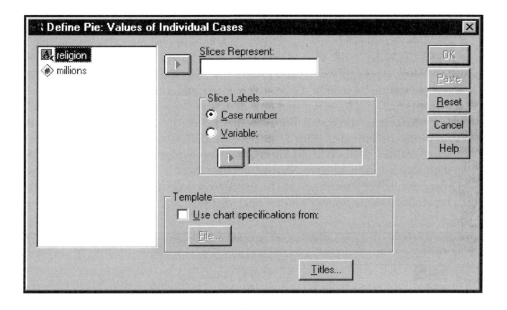

◆ The slices of the pie will obviously represent millions of worshippers, so click **millions** on the left and move it to the box labelled **Slices Represent** by clicking the upper arrow button. The religions are identified by names listed in a variable (column) in the Data Editor, and not merely by case numbers in the Data Editor, so in the Slice Labels group select **Variable** by clicking its radio button. Now you can move the variable **religion** on the left to the **Slice Labels: Variable** box by clicking it and then clicking the lower arrow button. Click **OK**, and the pie chart will appear in the SPSS Viewer.

◆ You can edit the pie chart by double-clicking it to enter the SPSS Chart Editor. You may then edit it by using the functions activated by the icon bar as outlined in section 13.2, or by double-clicking on features of the pie chart and using the dialog boxes that open immediately – and their help buttons if necessary.

◆ Put the mouse pointer among the labels of the slices on the left and double-click. In the Pie Options dialog box that opens click **Edit text...** to get to the subdialog box called Pie Options: Edit Text Labels. Select the label **Confuc** from the list by clicking it (use the scroll bar to find it), then click inside the **Label** box and edit it by typing the rest of the word so it becomes **Confucianism**, and click **Change**, then **Continue** to get back to the Pie Options dialog box. Change the label **Christan** in the same way by double-clicking it, opening the subdialog box called Pie Options: Edit Text Labels, typing

Christianity, then clicking **C**hange. Click **Continue** to get back to the Pie Options dialog box, then **OK**, and the chart in the SPSS Viewer will reappear with the full labels **Confucianism** and **Christianity**.

◆ Click the slice of the pie labelled **Buddhism** so that it is outlined in black, then click the Explode Slice icon – the icon that looks like a disc with an arrow pointing out from it, located fourth from last in the icon bar. The Buddhism slice will be separated slightly from the rest of the chart.

◆ If you're happy with the pie chart, click **F**ile in the menu bar, followed by **C**lose, and the SPSS Viewer will reappear with the edited chart. You could print it or save it, if you wished, using the procedure we explained in the last few paragraphs of section 13.2. Now you are going to turn the same data into a simple line graph.

◆ Click **G**raph in the menu bar near the top of the SPSS Viewer, and in the drop-down menu click **Line...**, and in the Line Charts dialog box that opens select **Values of individual cases** (for reasons already explained), then click the picture button labelled **Simple**, because there is only one variable and will therefore be only one line on the graph. Then click **Define**, and a subdialog box called Define Simple Line: Values of Individual Cases will open.

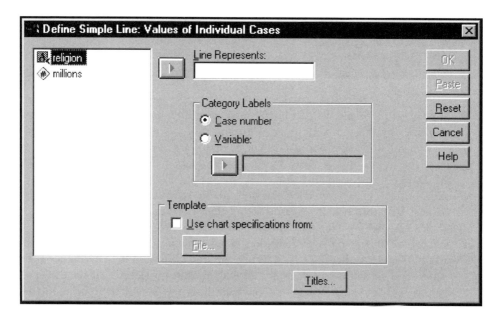

◆ In this subdialog box, move the variable name **millions** from the left to the box labelled **L**ine represents by clicking it and then clicking the upper arrow button. Because the religions are identified by names and not merely by case numbers in the Data Editor, in the Category Labels group select **V**ariable by clicking its radio button. Now you can move the variable name **religion** on the left to the **Category Labels: V**ariable box by clicking it and then clicking the lower arrow button. You could, if you wished, add a title, subtitle, and footnote by clicking **Titles...**, but instead, click **OK**, and the simple line graph will appear in the SPSS Viewer. You could, of course, have produced this graph directly, without drawing a pie chart first. You already know how to edit the labels on the simple line graph; in the next section we'll show you how to improve the appearance of a line graph in other ways.

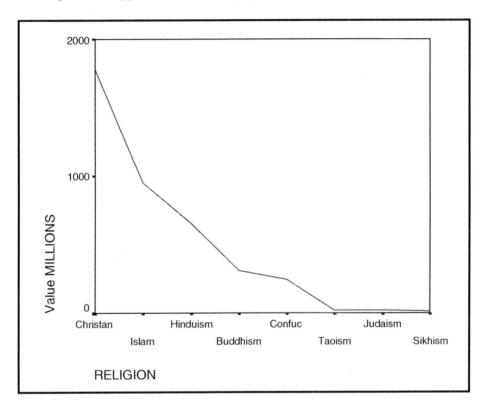

13.4 MULTIPLE LINE GRAPHS

You may well need to produce a graph with two or more lines on it, and for this you need to use the SPSS Multiple Line Chart facility. The results of multifactorial analysis of variance, for example, are often displayed graphically, especially if they include significant interactions that need to be interpreted. Let's create a graph to display the data from the multifactorial ANOVA that you carried out in chapter 10. But before you can do this, you may want to close the graphs currently in the SPSS Viewer.

◆ Click **File** in the menu bar near the top of the SPSS Viewer, then click **Close** in the menu that drops down. If you have not saved the output already, a warning will appear asking whether you want to do so. Click **Yes** if you do and **No** if you don't.

◆ In the Data Editor, click **File** in the menu bar that drops down, then **New**, then **Data**, and a dialog box will appear inviting you to save the data currently in the Data Editor. Click **Yes** if you want to save it (under the file name **religion.sav**) and **No** if you don't. Then click **File**, followed by **Open** in the menu, and the Open File dialog box will appear.

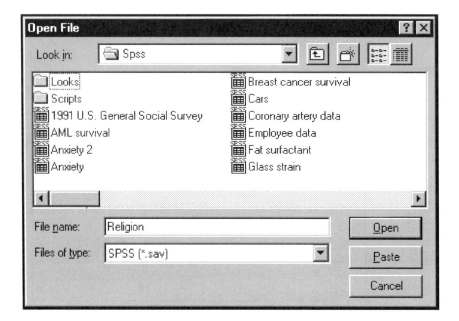

◆ Make sure that the disk containing data from chapter 10 is in the disk drive. If the box labelled **Look in** is not showing the drive in which you have the data, click the arrow on the right of the box and select the right drive, probably **3½ Floppy (A:)**, from the drop-down menu by clicking it.
◆ Find the data file **genaud**, using the scroll bars if some of the files have scrolled out of sight, click it so that its name appears in the **File name** box, then click **Open**. The input data from the Corston and Colman (1996) experiment on gender and audience effects on a computer tracking task will appear in the Data Editor.
◆ Click **Graphs** in the Data Editor, then click **Line...** in the drop-down menu, and the Line Charts dialog box that you have already seen will open again. This time, click the picture button labelled **Multiple**, because there have to be two lines on the graph in order to display the interaction effect.
◆ Click the radio button **Summaries for groups of cases**. We explained in section 13.2 that this is what you should select when you have cases (rows in the Data Editor) that fall into several subgroups, and that is exactly what you have in this instance – the grouping variables in the second and third columns show which groups the scores belong to. If the data that you wanted to display consisted of values or numbers associated with rows of the Data Editor, then

you would select **Values of individual cases**, and if you had a different variable in each column of the Data Editor, you would select **Summaries of separate variables**. Click **Define**, and a dialog box called Define Multiple Line: Summaries for Groups of Cases will open.

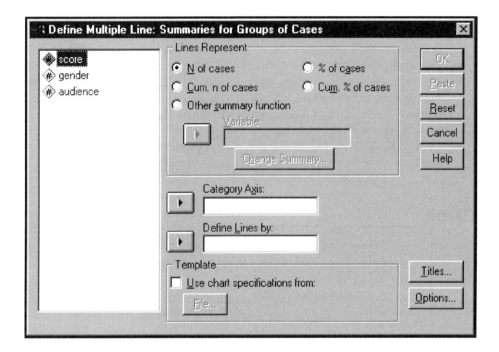

◆ The lines on the graph are obviously going to represent the dependent variable – the actual scores – so you have to move the variable name **score** from the left to the box in the group on the right labelled **Variable**, but the text box and its arrow button are dimmed and it isn't ready to accept the variable name. Furthermore, you want the lines to represent mean scores for the various treatment conditions, not **N of cases** or **Cum. n of cases**, or apparently any of the other options listed. Means are not listed, but if you first click the radio button labelled **Other summary function**, then the text box labelled **Variable** and its arrow button will spring to life, and when you move the variable name **score** to the box by clicking the upper arrow button it will appear there as **MEAN(score)**. Try to remember this because it's something you'd never guess, and people who don't know it get stuck at this point. If you wanted some other summary function rather than the means, such as medians or variances, you could click **Change Summary...** below it, and a dialog box would open in which you could select another function from a comprehensive list.

◆ By convention, the vertical axis of a graph normally represents values of the dependent variable, which in this case is **score**. Now decide which of the remaining two variables is to be the category variable represented along the horizontal axis and which is to be represented by different lines on the graph. This is an easy decision, because it is generally a good idea to have as few lines as possible on a graph, so the variable with the fewest values should normally be the one represented by different lines. Click the variable name **audience** on the left and transfer it to the box labelled **Category Axis**. Then click the variable name **gender** (which has only two values) on the left and transfer it to the box labelled **Define Lines by** clicking the arrow button pointing to that box.

◆ The dialog box has a button marked **Titles...** that opens a subdialog box in which you could, if you wished, add a title, subtitle, and footnote to your graph, as with other charts and graphs. It also has a button marked **Options...** that opens a dialog box in which you could specify the treatment of missing values, if you had any.

◆ Click **OK**, and the SPSS Viewer will appear with your interaction graph displayed once again (you saw a version of this graph in section 10.4).

Graph

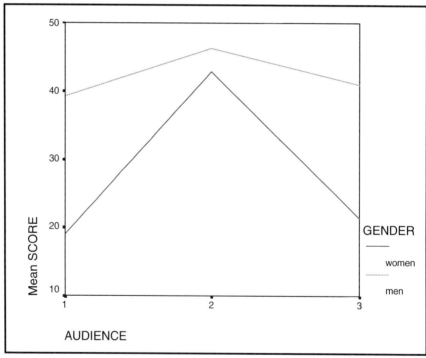

◆ Double-click the graph to transfer it to the Chart Editor. Change the label of the vertical axis from **Mean SCORE** to **COOPERATIVE CHOICES** and centre this label on its axis by double-clicking the label and editing it in the Scale Axis dialog box, as explained in section 13.2. Now double-click **AUDIENCE** and centre it on the horizontal axis in the same way.

◆ The lines on the graph would be hard to distinguish in black and white. This is something you can't alter by double-clicking. Click (once) the line representing women (make sure handles appear on it), then click the fifth icon (the horizontal broken line) in the second row of the Chart Editor's icon bar, and a dialog box for selecting line styles will appear.

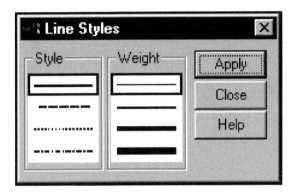

◆ Click the unbroken style on the left and the second-heaviest weight on the right, then click **Apply**, followed by **Close**. Do the same thing with the line representing men, but this time select a dashed line style on the left and the second-heaviest weight on the right, followed by **Apply**, then **Close**.

◆ A strange feature of SPSS for Windows is that the markers – the dots, triangles, circles, or other symbols to which the lines are connected – are normally suppressed. To add them to the graph, first click the line representing women, then click the Marker icon – the fourth icon in the second row of the icon bar. In the Markers dialog box that opens, select the round black dot by clicking it (it will be enclosed in a square), then select **Large** size, and finally click **Apply All**. Do the same thing to the line representing men, but select a large-sized black triangle, followed by **Close**. The markers will still not be visible on the graph.

◆ Click **Format** in the menu bar, then **Interpolation...**, and in the Line Interpolation dialog box that opens click **Straight** on the left. Put a tick in the check box beside **Display markers**. Click **Apply All**, followed by **Close**, and the markers will become visible on the screen. Not many people know how to do that.

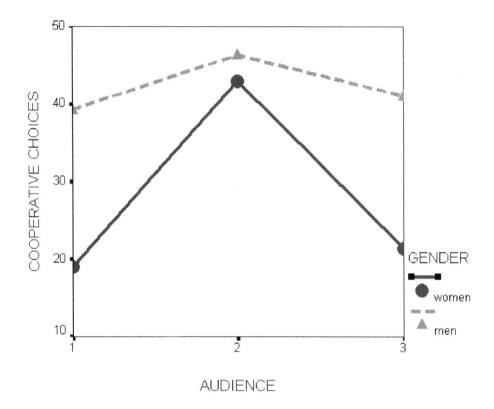

◆ Click **File** followed by **Close**, and you will be back in the SPSS Viewer. Your graph is now ready for printing and/or saving as before (see towards the end of section 13.2). It shows very vividly (or perhaps we should say very graphically) that men performed better at the computer tracking task than women, but that the female audience had a much stronger effect on the performance of women than on the performance of men, with approximately equal performance for men and women in the female audience condition. The interaction was statistically significant (see section 10.4), and the interaction graph shows what the interaction means more clearly and elegantly than the previous 56-word sentence.

13.5 SCATTERPLOTS

Scatterplots, also called scattergrams or scatter diagrams, are especially useful for interpreting correlations. We'll show you how to draw one to illustrate the data that we presented in section 5.2 on the relationship between the annual number of lynchings in the southern United States from 1882 to 1930 and the value of cotton production in the corresponding years. Before you can do this, you may want to close the graph currently in the Chart Editor window.

◆ Click **File** in the menu bar near the top of the SPSS Viewer, then click **Close** in the menu that drops down. If you have not saved the graph already, a dialog box will appear asking whether you want to do so. Click **Yes** if you do and **No** if you don't.

◆ Back in the Data Editor, click **File** in the menu bar, then **New**, then **Data**, and when a dialog box appears asking whether you want to save the current contents of the Data Editor, click **No**. Click **File** then **Open** in the drop-down menu, and the Open File dialog box will open. Make sure that the disk containing the data from chapter 5 is in the disk drive. If the box labelled **Look in** is not showing the drive in which you have the data, click the arrow on the right of the box and select the right drive, probably **3½ Floppy (A:)**, from the drop-down menu by clicking it.

◆ Find the data file **lynch**, using the scroll bars if some of the files have scrolled out of sight, click it so that its name appears in the **File name** box, then click **Open**. The input data from the Hovland and Sears (1940) study of lynching and cotton production will appear in the Data Editor.

◆ Click **Graphs** in the SPSS Viewer, then click **Scatter...** in the drop-down menu. The Scatterplot dialog box will open.

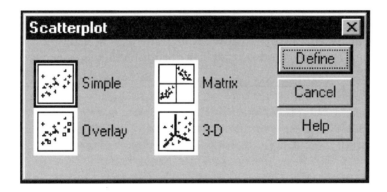

◆ Click the picture button labelled **Simple**. The other picture buttons are for more complex scattergrams. **Overlay** is for multiple scatterplots displayed simultaneously within the same frame; **Matrix** is used to display the pairwise correlations in a set of three or more variables – it produces a matrix of all the bivariate scatterplots formed from pairs of variables in the set; and **3-D** is to display the joint distribution of three variables.

◆ Click **Define**, and the Simple Scatterplot dialog box, of a type with which you are by now familiar, will open. Because of the convention of having the dependent variable on the vertical axis, you should put the number of lynchings on this axis. Click **lynch** on the left and move it to the box labelled **Y Axis** by clicking the upper arrow button, then use the same technique to move **cotton** to the box labelled **X Axis**.

◆ Ignore **Set Markers by**, which would allow you to use a different symbol for each value of the variable in the scatterplot. Ignore **Label Cases by**, which would allow you to label each point in the plot if it contained only a small number of points. Ignore **Template**, which would allow you to apply the specifications from a selected template to your own scatterplot.

◆ If you wished to add a title, subtitle, and/or footnote to your scatterplot, you could click <u>Titles...</u>, and a dialog box would open allowing you to type in the required text. If you had any missing values, you could specify how they should be treated by clicking **Options...** to open a dialog box for this purpose.

◆ Click **OK**, and the scatterplot will appear in the SPSS Viewer. Double-click in the middle of the scatterplot to transfer it to the Chart Editor.

◆ Double-click the word LYNCH on the vertical axis, and the Y Scale Axis dialog box, which you've seen before, will open. In the **Axis** <u>Title</u> text box, change the label **LYNCH** by clicking inside the box and typing **LYNCHINGS**. Click the arrow on the right of the **Title** <u>Justification</u> text box, and select **Center** from the drop-down menu by clicking it, then click **OK**. On the horizontal axis, change the label to **COTTON PRODUCTION** and centre it by double-clicking it and following the same procedure.

◆ Click the Marker icon – the fourth icon in the bottom row of the Chart Editor's icon bar. In the Markers dialog box that opens, select the round black dot by clicking it, then click the radio button labelled <u>Small</u>, and then click **Apply** <u>All</u>, followed by **Close**. Close the SPSS Viewer by clicking <u>File</u> in the menu bar, followed by <u>Close</u>. Your scatterplot is ready for printing and/or saving by the methods already described towards the end of section 13.2.

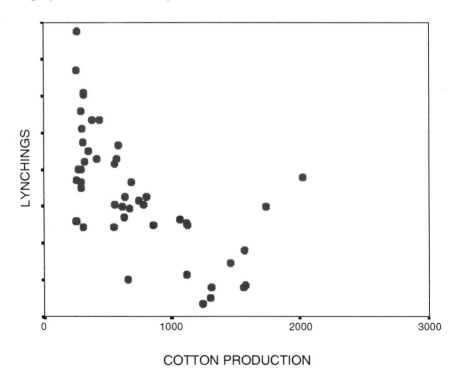

The scatterplot shows quite vividly how the number of lynchings tended to be highest in years in which the value of cotton production was lowest, and vice versa. It also shows that there were some exceptional years that did not follow this rule, despite the whopping negative correlation of −.64 between the two variables.

◆ Exit from SPSS by clicking **File** in the menu bar near the top of the SPSS Viewer, and then **Exit** at the bottom of the menu that drops down. If you have not saved the graph already, a warning will appear asking whether you want to do so. Click **Yes** if you do and **No** if you don't.

If you've reached this point in the book by working carefully through all the earlier chapters, then let us be the first to congratulate you. It would no longer be appropriate to describe you as a beginner, and you are probably already equipped to do most of the analyses that you require. You're entitled to feel quite pleased with yourself. If you have any comments or suggested improvements, then please send us an e-mail (rcorston@cwcom.net/amc@le.ac.uk) or write to us care of the publishers.

References

Cohen, S., Lichtenstein, E., Prochaska, J. O., Rossi, J. S., Gritz, E. R., Carr, C. R., Orleans, C. T., Schoenbach, V. J., Biener, L., Abrams, D., DiClementi, C., & Curry, S. (1989). Debunking myths about self-quitting: Evidence from 10 prospective studies of persons who attempt to quit smoking by themselves. *American Psychologist, 44*, 1355–1365.

Colman, A. M. (1982). *Game Theory and Experimental Games: The Study of Strategic Interaction*. Oxford: Pergamon.

Corston, R. & Colman, A. M. (1996). Gender and social facilitation effects on computer competence and attitudes toward computers. *Journal of Educational Computing Research, 14*, 171–183.

Fazio, R. H., Jackson, J. R., Dunton, B. C., & Williams, C. J. (1995). Variability in automatic activation as an unobtrusive measure of racial attitudes: A bona fide pipeline. *Journal of Personality and Social Psychology, 69*, 1013–1027.

Feller, W. (1968). *An Introduction to Probability Theory and its Applications* (3rd ed., Vol. 1). New York: Wiley.

Hays, W. L. (1994). *Statistics* (5th ed.). Fort Worth, TX: Harcourt Brace.

Henderson, E. & Allan, W. (1994). *Collins Gem Fact File*. Glasgow: HarperCollins.

Hovland, C. I. & Sears, R. R. (1940). Minor studies of aggression: VI. Correlation of lynchings with economic indices. *Journal of Psychology, 9*, 301–310.

Howell, D. C. (1999). *Fundamental Statistics for the Behavioral Sciences* (4th ed.). Pacific Grove, CA: Duxbury Press.

Huck, S. W. & Cormier, W. H. (1996). *Reading Statistics and Research* (2nd ed.). New York: HarperCollins.

Juel-Nielsen, N. (1965). Individual and environment: A psychiatric-psychological investigation of monozygous twins reared apart. *Acta Psychiatrica et Neurologica Scandinavica*, Monograph Supplement 183.

Knox, V. J., Morgan, A. H., & Hilgard, E. R. (1974). Pain and suffering in ischemia: The paradox of hypnotically suggested anesthesia as contradicted by reports from the "hidden observer". *Archives of General Psychiatry, 30*, 840–847.

Norušis, M. J. (1993). *SPSS for Windows Base System User's Guide Release 6.0*. Chicago, IL: SPSS Inc.

Pagano, R. R. (1998). *Understanding Statistics in the Behavioral Sciences* (5th ed.). Pacific Grove, CA: Brooks/Cole.

Universities Funding Council. (1993). *A Report for the Universities Funding Council on the Conduct of the 1992 Research Assessment Exercise*. Bristol: Author.

Index